Crisis in the pulpit

Crisis in the pulpit

The pulpit faces future shock

Chevis F. Horne

BAKER BOOK HOUSE
Grand Rapids, Michigan

Library of Congress Catalog Card Number: 74-20203
ISBN: 0-8010-4108-2

TO
HELEN, CHIP, AND ANN
who knowing me as I really am
love and accept me

FOREWORD

AFTER MORE THAN A QUARTER OF A CENTURY OF SERVICE IN A parish in Virginia, Dr. Horne has given us in this volume a discerning view of the problems and possibilities in pulpit preaching in the 70s. Out of his own experience and a broad acquaintance with the literature in the field, he presents a strong case for the future of the pulpit ministry, in full awareness of the crisis facing the future of the institutional church and its preaching.

Holding firmly to the heart of the gospel and the necessity of reaching the individual in terms of his own personal anxiety and failures in a world of devastatingly rapid change, he is sensitive to the individual's entanglement in the complex and often frightening social, economic, and political issues of today. He sees the ministry of the church as an enabling ministry for laymen to carry the full gospel to the world in which they live. He sees the pulpit as a primary element in that enabling ministry. For the preacher, this means an often agonizing identification with the man in the pew in his doubts and uncertainties and in his wrestling with the tangled ethical decision involved not only in his personal life but in his life in a world torn by the problems of race, war, poverty, and ecology.

To read *Crisis in the Pulpit* is to enter into the personal record of one pastor's own struggle with the place of preaching in today's world. It reads almost like a diary into which a man has poured out his strong Biblical faith and the inevitable conflict which ensues as he attempts to discover the meaning of that faith for a secular and revolutionary world. There is no question that Dr. Horne takes his

Bible seriously, the world seriously, and the attempt to bring the two together in preaching, seriously. His book is a record of the struggle which should be going on in the soul of any man who is called to preach the Gospel in the 70s.

Edmund A. Steimle

CONTENTS

Foreword 7

Introduction 11

1. Facing a Crisis in Preaching 15

2. The Focus of Preaching 23

3. Making the Gospel Personal 31

4. The Personal Cross in Preaching 39

5. Preaching Where People Are 47

6. Communicating the Gospel 55

7. Letting the Sermon Be Empowered 63

8. Preaching Within the Church 71

9. Preaching Beyond the Church 81

10. Preaching to Individual Man 91

11. Preaching to Corporate Man 101

12. Preaching the Full Gospel to the Whole Man 111

13. Preaching to Men of Power 119

14. Preaching to Secular Man 129

15. Preaching to Cosmic Man 139

INTRODUCTION

A BOOK THAT SEEKS TO DEAL HONESTLY WITH CONTEMPORARY preaching must face an obvious fact: There is a crisis in the pulpit. It is crucial. It may well be the most serious pulpit crisis in the whole history of the church. This is a sobering fact, and foolish is the preacher who does not take seriously the present crisis of preaching.

The crisis of the pulpit, rather than being simple, is very complex. It has resulted from the converging of four other crises: faith, the institutional church, authority, and communication.

In facing the crisis of modern preaching, one must be realistic. I have begun where I think a book of this kind must begin—with the crisis about which I have been speaking. The first chapter is entitled: "Facing a Crisis in Preaching." The rest of the book is written in the awareness of the crisis and in an effort to show how preaching can be more effective.

Having honestly faced the crisis, the preacher must be sure of the focus of his preaching. What is the heart of the gospel he preaches? He will find it in God's saving act in Jesus Christ, set in a long history of God's redemptive action.

The preacher must look at himself. If the pulpit is to be renewed in our time, the person who occupies it will have more to do with its renewal than anyone else. How will the gospel become a personal reality for him? How will the cross of Jesus, which in a sense is the most crucial event of the gospel, find a counterpart in his own life?

11

It is only as the gospel becomes real to him that he can speak with living authority. But if this has happened to him, he can speak with living authority. His hearers will know that they are being confronted with reality.

Having looked seriously at the gospel he is to preach as well as at himself, he must be sensitively aware of the people to whom he will preach. God's saving action in Jesus Christ was for people, and the preacher must seek to reach people where they are with the gospel. At the risk of using an overworked word, his preaching must be relevant. He must know where people always stand as well as the shifting positions of the present moment. He must know how to communicate the gospel to them in a way that will grip them, and he must be able to lay hold of sources of power that lie beyond him.

Preaching is a function of the church through the preacher, and the gospel must be addressed to the church and the world beyond the church. The preacher must help the church to keep its integrity, identity, and sense of unique mission, and at the same time to be vitally in touch with the world where its life is set. And he must help its members to grow to Christian maturity. But he must always be aware of the larger world. How will he help equip his church so that the laity can carry the gospel into the world? He is confronted with no more serious question than this.

The preacher must address the gospel to men, both in their individual and corporate life. To neglect either is to neglect a basic side of man's existence as well as to fail to preach a basic facet of the gospel. He must be careful to speak the full gospel to the whole man.

The modern preacher must preach to men who are greatly influenced by secularity, who are very conscious of power and achievement, yet are frightened and unsure of their future. Unless he can preach a gospel of power, offering redemption and hope, he will feel like a midget preaching to giants. Such a gospel he has.

Man in the last few years has been freed of his earth-boundness. He can now go beyond the atmosphere and gravitational field of his earth. He has gone to the moon and will go to other planets in his solar system. He has emerged as cosmic man. It is, therefore, the modern preacher's privilege and challenge to preach the cosmic Christ to cosmic man.

While preaching during a time of crisis in the pulpit, one need not despair. This is not the first crisis of the pulpit and it will not be the last. Preaching has survived others, and it has resources, if properly used, to survive this one. That is hope. Indeed, preaching can emerge that will be more authentic and compelling than we have known in our time.

1 / FACING A CRISIS IN PREACHING

THE MODERN PREACHER MUST FACE THE FACT THAT THERE IS A crisis in preaching. It is not the first crisis the pulpit has faced. Every generation has had its prophets of doom who bemoaned the loss of influence of the pulpit. Some have even predicted the demise of preaching. But the present crisis may be the most serious preaching has had to face in the whole history of the church.

An influential churchman, Marcus Dods, at the close of the nineteenth century was very perceptive when he wrote, "I do not envy those who will carry the banner of Christianity in the twentieth century . . . yes, perhaps I do, but it will be a stiff fight."[1] Dods was right, and possibly no area in the life of the church is more sensitive to the present crisis of Christianity than the pulpit.

D. W. Cleverley Ford has said that "preaching seems to be out of tune with the times. It doesn't fit the nineteen-seventies. Technological man has no ears for it. These opinions are what constitute the modern objections to preaching, and it stems not so much from focus outside the Church as from friends within it."[2]

The crisis of the pulpit has been produced by four converging crises: faith, the institutional church, authority, and communication.

Crisis of Faith

Preaching takes place within the context of faith. It declares

---

1. Wallace E. Fisher, *Preaching and Parish Renewal* (Nashville, New York: Abingdon Press, 1966), p. 21
2. D. W. Cleverly Ford, *Preaching Today* (London: Epworth Press & S.P.C.K., 1969), p. 2

God's saving action, especially in Jesus Christ, to which men respond by faith and trust. A crisis of faith, of necessity, produces a crisis in the pulpit. Such a crisis is on us! This is the most fundamental of the four crises with which we are here concerned.

Dietrich Bonhoeffer, the victim of Hitler's concentration camp who has had such a powerful influence on modern theology, spoke of how God is being edged out of modern life. "It is becoming evident," he wrote, "that everything gets along without 'God' and just as well as before. As in the scientific field, so in human affairs generally, what we call 'God' is being more and more edged out of life, losing more and more ground."[3]

As God was being edged out more and more, man was being pushed more and more to the center of life. Bonhoeffer spoke of man having come of age. Just as a child grows up and becomes independent of his parents, so modern man has grown up. He must not depend on a fatherly God. He must assume full responsibility for himself, his world, and his destiny. Therefore, Bonhoeffer saw man becoming progressively irreligious. He wrote: "We are proceeding towards a time of no religion at all: men as they are now simply cannot be religious anymore."[4]

It is easy to misunderstand Bonhoeffer. We must understand the kind of God who was being edged out of life. He was the God of metaphysics, dogma, liturgy, holy places, and holy times; the God who was on the borders of man's weakness and life's extremity; the God who moved into life like a rescue squad; the God of the stopgap who was used by man to fill the gaps made by his incomplete knowledge. Modern man, in giving up this kind of God, will become irreligious. But Bonhoeffer believed in a God who was in the midst of life, not so much in the cloister as in the world. This God is met and known as a man identifies with the weakness of life and shares the suffering of his world. Man knows God as he takes seriously the cross. "God is weak and powerless in the world," he wrote, "and that is exactly the way, the only way, in which he can be with us, and help us."[5] "It is not some religious act which makes a Christian what he is, but participation in the suffering of God in the life of

---

3. Dietrich Bonhoeffer, *Letters and Papers from Prison* (New York: The Macmillan Co., 1953), p. 195
4. Ibid., p. 162
5. Ibid., pp. 219-220

the world."[6] He was pleading for a worldly understanding of God that could be understood by secular man who had come of age.

Bonhoeffer was prophetic. Secular man has appeared full grown. And while he seems not to find God in the world as Bonhoeffer had hoped, he becomes progressively irreligious as Bonhoeffer predicted. He sees himself at the center of life, not God. His faith is in his own powers that have created his science, technology, education and social strategy. There is little or no sense of the transcendent in life.

The loss of God has cast a shadow of doubt over other tenets of his faith as traditionally understood. Jesus Christ is often reduced to an ethical image. For many he is the man for others rather than the strong Son of God. There is a lessening sense of sin and guilt, and, therefore, less conscious need for forgiveness and redemption. With a loss of the eternal dimension, there is loss of faith in eternal life. What happens, happens here and now. Man had better make the best of this life and this world.

The most radical expression of the crisis of faith has appeared in the radical theology of just a few years ago, popularly known as the God-is-dead theology. The radical theology completely lost the vertical dimension of faith. Everything was flattened out into human, ethical, and social concern. "What they are saying," writes Langdon Gilkey, "is that there is no God anywhere; the cosmos is stripped bare of such a divine being, or such a divine source of being. It is not that God is hiding, or beyond our experience; it is that the total universe is made up of rocks, stars, and beetles, and nothing at all like God is there or ever has been there."[7]

What is so startling is not that the radical theology has happened, but that it occured within the church. It happened within the church, the fellowship of faith. Its exponents occupied chairs of religion and preached from pulpits. When such dramatic and radical loss of faith happens outside the church, we are neither shocked nor surprised. But that this radical loss of faith appeared in such an articulate and systematic way within the fellowship of faith, is a first in the history of the church. It had never happened before.

The fact that the radical theology occurred within the church

---

6. Ibid., p. 223
7. Langdon Gilkey, *Naming the Whirlwind: The Renewal of God-Language* (Indianapolis and New York: The Bobbs-Merrill Co., 1969), p. 112

must give every preacher pause for serious thought. It didn't occur within a vacuum, but within a church which obviously had suffered a severe erosion of faith. It is true that not many within the church went to such extremes. They saw the inconsistency of the radical theology: How can you have a theology without God? Yet, the mass of church membership does not escape influence from the probing and serious questions that lie back of such a radical position. Every preacher must realize that increasingly he will preach to people who come, not only to make affirmations about faith but to receive help with serious questions and doubts. They hope the preacher can help them lift ceilings of life that are oppressively low, again opening up dimensions of height and mystery. They come from a crisis of faith.

Crisis of the Church

There is also a crisis of the institutional church. Many say they find an increasing attraction in Jesus but a growing alienation from the church. Since preaching is one of the basic functions of the church, the pulpit suffers proportionately in the crisis. Where there is a loss of faith in the integrity of the church, as there is in our day, there is a loss of faith in the integrity of preaching. The pulpit suffers from a credibility gap.

But why this loss of faith in the integrity of the church? Several reasons are evident:

First, some say that the church is introverted, that it turns in upon its own life, and that it is more concerned with serving itself than serving the world. The church is really a servant, existing not for itself but the world, but it seems to have forgotten that. It is bent on saving itself, not the world. This is one of the criticisms Bonhoeffer made of the church. "During these years the church has fought for self-preservation as though it were an end in itself, and has thereby lost its chance to speak a word of reconciliation to mankind and the world at large."[8]

Second, the charge of irrelevance is leveled at the church. It is not in touch with real life and its crucial issues. It has been tethered too closely to sacred buildings and holy hours. It has not freed itself to be the church in the world. It has often preached a theology that is abstract and withdrawn from life. It has been more con-

---

8. Op. cit., p. 187

cerned about saving souls than the redemption of the whole life and society.

During a time when fierce storms rage on the high seas, the church has too often sought the safety of quiet harbors. It has been timid rather than bold, failing frequently to speak with a clear voice on crucial issues like war, business morals, conflicts between labor and management, and the sexual revolution. It has been slow to effect positive social change, frequently being reactionary and defending the status quo. Rather than being a strong engine helping to pull the positive forces of social action, it has been a caboose, by and large, being pulled by them.

Third, the church reflects too much the spirit of its culture and too little the spirit of its Lord. Its gospel, too frequently, has been that of its culture, which has its source in democracy, national hope, and an optimistic view of man, rather than the Christian gospel which has its source in God's saving action in Christ. Rather than being controlled by the mind of Christ, it has embodied the values, standards, and fragmentation of its society. The church, like its Lord, is to be a servant, but it has sought power, prestige, and status symbols not unlike those of its culture.

Paul, especially in his Ephesian letter, sees a new humanity that has healed old wounds, transcended old barriers, and united separated and hostile men. The sphere of the new humanity is to be the church, the body of Christ. Yet, the church is so far from being that new humanity. Racism has made one of its last ditch stands in the church, and the social stratification of our society is reflected more clearly in it than most places. It is broken like the world, and lacks the wholeness God intends.

Crisis of Authority

Rebellion against authority runs the full length of our cultural spectrum. There is obvious rebellion against authority in all our institutions—government, the home, the school, and the church. This is one of the marks of our times. Since the church is not being spared, the pulpit cannot be spared either.

But the pulpit is particularly sensitive to rebellion against authority. And that for a very obvious reason: it has been very authority conscious. No center of life has laid claim to a more ultimate authority than the pulpit. It has been able to say, "Thus saith the Lord." The preacher claims to speak the word of God.

Back of him has been an authority no less than that of God. But every preacher must realize now that there are those in his congregation who question some of the things he says, or disagree with him outright.

There are two basic reasons for a rebellion against authority in the pulpit. The first is modern man's claim for his freedom. He considers this an inalienable birthright. He feels capable of finding truth for himself, establishing his values, ordering his own life, and locating authority within himself. Langdon Gilkey has commented on this: "Thus the modern spirit, at least in the West, is dedicated to the proposition that any external authority—whether of church, of state, of local community, or of family—will in the end only crush man's humanity if his own personal being does not participate fully and voluntarily in whatever help that authority represents and in whatever creative forms his life may take."[9]

The stress on freedom and reaction against authority explain, in part at least, dialogical preaching in our time. Many see the monological discourse of the pulpit as having had its day. Preaching must be dialogical. There must be an exchange between the pulpit and the pew. Authority must not only come down from the preacher. It must rise up from the congregation as well. Canon John V. Taylor has been bold to predict: 'But the old unquestioned monologue of the pulpit is less appropriate to our searching and tentative age than the interchange of discussion. More and more we ought to expect group study and exploration to do in our day what the sermon has done in the past."[10]

The second reason for rebellion against authority in the pulpit is relativism. Secular man no longer believes in absolutes. Everything is relative. Everything is conditioned and fashioned by its time and place. What is true in one situation may not be true in another. What is right in one situation may not be right in another. Everything is "determined in large part by all that lies behind it, shaped by all that surrounds it, and will be replaced by what follows. . . . Nothing anywhere in experience, space, time, or any mode of being is, in that sense, absolute; all is relative to all else and so essentially conditioned by its relevant environment."[11]

The pulpit has often dealt with absolutes, both theological and

9. Op. cit., p. 59
10. Ford, Op. cit., p. 2
11. Gilkey, op. cit., p. 48

ethical. Theologically, it has said that there is no way to God except through Jesus Christ and that no other name has been given by which man can be saved. Ethically, it has often said that the Ten Commandments are binding on all men everywhere, and at all times; or that love is an ethical absolute. The spirit of relativism challenges these claims.

Even the devout have not escaped the spirit of relativism. They sometimes ask serious questions about the absolutes they hear from the pulpit. I know a man who gives generously to missions but secretly wonders, while Christ is better for the United States, whether Confucius may not be better for China and Allah better for the Moslem world. This kind of person may be in our congregations more frequently than we know.

Crisis of Communication

Like the crisis of authority, the crisis of communication runs the full spectrum of our culture. We hear much about the generation gap existing between adults and young people. There is a communication gap often between parent and child, teacher and pupil, government and citizen. And there is a communication gap between the pulpit and pew. The pulpit is especially sensitive to the communication crisis since preaching is a basic form of communication within the church. Preaching, by its very nature, is communication.

Amos Wilder speaks of communication as being one of the main concerns of the church today, especially as it relates to preaching. "The preacher we are told is like a man speaking into a dead microphone. We hear on all sides about the need for the modernization of the Christian message, translation of the ancient image, the rediscovery of effective media of discourse."[12]

There seem to be at least three things that contribute to the communication crisis of the pulpit. First, its language often seems strange, abstract, and complex. Laymen do not understand the technical theological language frequently used; it is lacking in vividness, color, concreteness, and dramatic quality. Dull and abstract language falls upon listless ears.

Second, preaching depends on verbal communication at a time when visual communication seems to be in ascendancy in our

---

12. Amos N. Wilder, *The Language of the Gospel* (New York and Evanston: Harper and Row, 1964), p. 10

culture. We are bombarded with visual images on every side— television, newspapers, and journals that pictorialize their ideas, and advertising that makes most effective use of visual communication. Verbal communication often seems dull, prosaic, and unimaginative. Therefore, the church, more and more, makes use of visual arts in its worship: drama, the interpretive dance, and other visual media. These become instruments of worship. We put increasing faith in visual communication. Preaching suffers.

Third, preaching deals with realities that seem strange to secular, empirical, and scientific man. It talks about the supernatural, the spiritual, and the intangible. These cannot be proved by the scientific method nor tested in the laboratory. This is obviously related to the crisis of faith. God-language speaks of realities that seem strange and unreal and, therefore, is often unintelligible.

Foolish is the preacher who is not aware of the crisis of the pulpit. He should take it most seriously. Yet, he should not despair. While this may be the most serious crisis in preaching so far, it is not the first and will not be the last. Preaching has survived other crises and it will survive this one. Preaching proclaims God's saving action, and man cannot live without hearing this good news.

2 /
THE FOCUS
OF PREACHING

DURING A TIME OF CRISIS IN THE PULPIT, THE PREACHER MUST BE sure of the focus of his preaching. The focus of preaching is God's redemptive action for us men in Jesus Christ.

James S. Stewart has put it this way: "Therefore settle it with your souls that, whatever else you may do or leave undone, you will preach in season and out of season God's redemptive deed in Christ."[1] Kyle Haselden has reminded us that "the gospel we were appointed to preach is a blunt, unapologetic claim that Jesus Christ is the Light of the world—timeless, universal, final, sufficient."[2] And Paul, the greatest of preachers, declared that ". . . I determined not to know anything among you, save Jesus Christ, and him crucified." (I Cor. 2:2).

The focus of preaching must not be blurred, and Jesus Christ must be seen clearly against a background of a long series of saving events. And He must be seen in relation to other truths that radiate from Him as center. He will be the touchstone by which we judge all spiritual reality.

As preachers we are called upon to be many things to many men. We are called upon always to preach Jesus Christ. He is the focus of our preaching.

1. James S. Stewart, *Heralds of God* (New York: Charles Scribner's Sons, 1946), p. 69
2. Kyle Haselden, *The Urgency of Preaching* (New York, Evanston, London: Harper and Row, 1963), p. 67

His Full Life

We must preach the full life of Jesus Christ—birth, childhood, adult life, death, resurrection, ascension, and His authority as living Lord.

At the birth of Jesus, God made a strange, new entrance into human history. There the "Word was made flesh." His birth cleaved history; humanity was given a new start. We put forth some of our best efforts in music, pageantry, and art to tell of this decisive event.

We must preach His childhood, although that period is known as the silent years. Yet, we know one important thing about those early years: His life unfolded in a normal pattern. He grew as other normal children. Therefore, children everywhere can identify with him.

His adult years were marked by love and service.

The motives of the best men are always mixed and muddled. But the motives of Jesus were crystal clear. He knew a pure, unbroken love. His was a love that completely gave itself, asked for nothing in return, and laid no claim upon the person loved. Only after men made a free response to Him did Jesus press His claims of Lordship over them. His love was not dependent upon the goodness, beauty, worthiness, and achievement of a person. He loved the sinful, broken, ugly, and repulsive with an unsparing love. It is little wonder that Jesus defined great religion in terms of love of God and neighbor, and gave to us an ethic of love.

But the love of Jesus was not blind and sentimental. Although He was not a judge, there was judgment in His love. It was like the judgment of light over darkness and truth over falsehood. His love was a searching light that exposed the darkness of men's pride, greed, false ambition, and sin.

The love of Jesus pointed straight to the nature of God. So men, after Him, could define God as a God of love. Despite the blind, impersonal, capricious forces of our universe, men could believe that love is at the heart of reality.

The love of Jesus expressed itself in servanthood. It is the nature of love to serve, to be servant and not master. Jesus was offered a crown but He asked for a towel and basin of water. Greatness lay, not in mastering men, but in serving them. The great among His followers, therefore, would be they who were the servants of men. The early church could not forget that Jesus Christ became a servant. Paul remembered how He took upon Himself "the form of a servant" (Phil. 2:7).

The light that shone in His face threatened the darkness that was in men's minds. They could not tolerate Him. Powerful forces set themselves against Him early in His ministry and dogged His footsteps to the end. He walked resolutely in the shadow of the cross, which fell across His path almost from the beginning of His public life, until He was nailed to that instrument of death. This servant of men, in His death as well as His life, fulfilled Isaiah's image of the Suffering Servant. He who took upon Himself the form of a servant "humbled himself and became obedient unto death, even the death on a cross" (Phil. 2:8).

But death could not contain this giver of life. Three days after Jesus' death, God bared His mighty arm and brought Him forth from the dead. Quickly the good news spread: He is risen!

Beyond the empty tomb is ascension, when Jesus Christ freed Himself from the limitation of space and time. The New Testament speaks of Him as being at the right hand of the Father, which means that He is at the place of sovereign power. Yet, the authority and power of the exalted Lord is not obvious in our world. His followers live in a world where power is often ruthless, careless of human welfare and dignity, and so they are often forced to live in structures of life that are careless of Jesus' ethic of love. The church, which is His body, is not spared this ambiguity. Yet by faith, the power and authority of our living Lord are seen. We are sure that the tedious years of man's history move toward Christ and that someday He will step forth from His position of hidden power and consummate history. Then His sovereign power will be obvious to all. "One day the hour will strike when the King will lay aside His beggar's robes, in order to show His royal glory."[3]

Death and Resurrection

We are to preach the full life of Jesus Christ. Yet, His death and resurrection have special significance. Paul saw the gospel as a kind of ellipse with the death and resurrection of Jesus as the two foci. "For I delivered to you as of first importance," Paul wrote the church at Corinth, "what I also received, that Christ died for our

---

3. Emil Brunner, *Revelation and Reason* (Philadelphia: The Westminster Press, 1946), p. 187

sins in accordance with the scriptures, that he was buried, that he was raised on the third day in accordance with the scriptures" (I Cor. 15:3-4, RSV).

At the cross of Jesus, sin is more mercilessly exposed than anywhere else. Yet, at the cross, vulgar, and obvious sins are not exposed so much as the subtle, refined, and respectable ones. Theft, robbery, prostitution, and murder do not need to be exposed since they expose themselves. But sins that wear cloaks of respectability are disrobed at the cross and left in their stark, ugly nakedness.

Jesus was not put to death by hoodlums and gangsters. No, the forces of respectability crucified Him. Church and state, the custodians of religion and justice joined hands in doing away with Him. We see, at the cross, not how bad bad men are but how bad "good" men can be. There is where the proud and respectable man must cry out: "Lord, be merciful to me a sinner."

If a hoodlum had stabbed Jesus to death in a back alley, the authorities would have called it murder. But since respectable forces put Him to death in due process of the law, they called it justice. But before God, and now in the sight of history, the hearts of Caiaphas and the other accusers were just as murderous as that of a hoodlum who might have stabbed Him to death.

Here is revealed one of the greatest tragedies of human history. While man's achievements in justice, goodness, and morality, are often impressive and praiseworthy, he builds into his most respectable structures his pride, egotism and insecurity. Because he does, these structures often become forces of oppression, exploitation, and injustice.

Not only was sin exposed at the cross of Jesus, but evil was crippled there. Evil overly extended itself at the cross. It went too far. There truth engaged falsehood, humility engaged pride, and love engaged hate in a way known nowhere else in history. There evil was mortally wounded. While still powerful, evil must forever go limping until God utterly destroys it. Yet, the New Testament recognizes it as being formidable and powerful. Man's engagement with it is never a sham battle. The battle is real and the casualities are high. But in the New Testament there is not the slightest suggestion that evil can win.

A man who went on a safari in Africa remembers mortally wounding an elephant. Though fatally injured, the animal seemed to be more furious and powerful than ever before. But he was doomed. Just so with evil. The victory over it has already been won, despite the fact that it is still powerful and destructive.

But that is not the whole story. Not only is sin exposed and evil crippled at the cross of Jesus, there sin is forgiven. There a man is wrested from alien hands that have enslaved him, and given back to the hands that should really possess him. There a man is set right with his God. There he can be forgiven, restored, and redeemed.

This is possible because in the cross of Christ is the love that loves to the uttermost, the grace that accepts the worst, and the mercy that heals the sickest. There is where man's shame is absorbed, his guilt carried, and his pain borne. There are the stripes that heal us.

In the resurrection, Jesus Christ has won over death which is man's last and most dreaded enemy. The tomb, which is a symbol of man's ultimate defeat and imprisonment, has had its seal broken on Easter morning. It has been robbed of its glory. Christian faith has not only a cross, but an empty tomb set against a breaking day.

There is an invincible sense of victory in the New Testament. It has many sources but its chief source is the resurrection. The funeral dirge has given way to a mighty shout of victory. "O death, where is thy sting? O grave, where is thy victory?" (I Cor. 15:55).

And there is great joy in the New Testament. In none of the world's literature is joy so irrepressible, and, like the strong sense of victory, its source is in the resurrection more than anywhere else.

This joy will not be suppressed. You might as well command the incoming tide to recede as to try to suppress that joy. You could as well hold back the light of dawn by throwing up a canvas on your back porch against the morning as hold back that joy.

The death and resurrection of Jesus Christ must be held together. They are only three days apart historically. They are even closer in faith. They are like two sides of the same event. To say cross, is to say empty tomb. To say death, is to say resurrection. To say Christ crucified, is to say Christ resurrected.

Without the resurrection, the cross would be a pitiable tragedy. If history bothered to remember it at all, it would remember it as tragedy. It would be just another case, of which there are many, of goodness being overpowered and destroyed by evil.

I remember talking about the meaning of Good Friday to a group of children. A little girl commented: "Why call it Good

Friday? What's good about it? Everything that happened that day
was bad. Why not call it Bad Friday?" And that is what it would
be without Easter. The resurrection took that which would have
been sheer tragedy and turned it into mighty victory.

But it is the cross that makes sure the resurrection is something more than a display of sheer power. The Jesus who was
crucified because He loved men so was the same Jesus who was
resurrected. At the empty tomb, God did more than bare His
mighty arm. He bared his mighty, loving heart as well. But we
would not have known that without the cross.

As Saviour and Lord

We must preach Jesus Christ as both Saviour and Lord.

Man needs forgiveness because he is a sinner. He has a cleft
will and that cleft is down the center of his will. He is self-centered
and rebellious. Given ways of light, he chooses to walk in darkness. Man's problem is not so much that he does not know what is
right as that he is unable to perform it. He has a sick will. Because
of rebellious and false choices, he is separated from God and his
brother. He needs someone who can forgive his sins and overcome
his estrangement through reconciliation.

There is not health in man to heal his sickness nor power to
overcome his separation. He cannot speak the word of forgiveness.
He is helpless like the paralytic, borne by four men and let down
through the roof of a house at the feet of Jesus. Jesus looked at
him and said, "Son, thy sins be forgiven thee" (Mark 2:5). That is
what every man needs to hear. Only Christ can speak that word.

He who forgives man's sin and reconciles him to God has the
right to control him. Paul would introduce himself like this: "I
Paul, a slave of Jesus Christ." The earliest confession of Christian
faith was: Jesus Christ is Lord! That is still at the heart of Christian confession. Jesus Christ presses an absolute claim upon the life
He has forgiven.

The Christian gives a conditioned allegiance to everything—
state, school, church, even family, except Jesus Christ. To Him an
unconditional loyalty and a final obedience is given.

His Humanity and Divinity

We must preach Jesus Christ as being both human and divine.
That is the way the New Testament sees Him.

Jesus Christ was thoroughly human. You see Him as a baby dependent on his mother. He likely whimpered through that first Christmas night. We catch fleeting glimpses of Him during His childhood and adolescent years. We see Him more clearly as a young man. He was a carpenter, and later became a pedestrian teacher. His hands were calloused by the use of carpenter tools, and His face was bronzed by the sun. Sweat was on His face during a hot, sultry day in Nazareth. He grew tired and rested on the curbing of a well. He fell asleep in the bow of a ship with His head resting on a seaman's pillow. He arose from a night of sleep, refreshed and invigorated for a day of hard work. He was tempted. He became angry. He wept beside the grave of a friend. He was depressed in a garden where He prayed. He was crucified on a Roman cross, and blood, like that of any other man, oozed from His hands and side.

Whenever the humanity of Jesus has been attacked, authentic Christian faith has defended it. The New Testament, facing an early heresy called Gnosticism, that denied the humanity of Jesus, used some of its most vigorous language in the defense of His humanity.

The New Testament, also, sees Jesus Christ as being divine. It sees God acting and speaking through this man as in no other man of history. He was the Son of God.

Whenever men ask what God is like, we point to Jesus Christ. God is like Him. Jesus is the supreme revealer of God.

God sometimes seems far away and is like a cosmic blur. Jesus Christ throws God into focus. The blur begins to clear, lines begin to form, and a picture appears. The focus, however, is not on a cosmic screen but in the face of Jesus Christ. He could say: "He who has seen me has seen the Father" (John 14:9, RSV).

A missionary had worked with natives for many years. He had loved them, accepted them, and served them the way Jesus Christ loved, accepted, and served men. The natives, though simple like children, sensed the reality of Christ in this man's life. Then the day came when the missionary had to leave them and go home. The natives crowded about him to tell of their love and appreciation, and in their simple and unaffected way they said, "Sir, you have brought us God." We say that about Jesus Christ, yet in a much more profound and ultimate sense. He has brought us God.

Because Jesus Christ has brought us God, we are no longer under the intolerable burden of making our way to God. Christ says to us, "I am close to you, and I am close to God. By faith, put your hand into my hand and I will lead you to God." So the religious quest, which may have begun in strenuous effort, ends with God finding us in Jesus Christ.

In preaching the humanity and divinity of Jesus Christ, we must steer clear of an artificial and mechanical interpretation of His person. We must not picture Him as shifting gears between the human and divine within His life. There was a wholeness, a one-ness, a unity about his person. We must be modest about our claims to understand intellectually his humanity and divinity. There is mystery there. Reverence and modesty, therefore, will be more be-coming of us than intellectual arrogance and a dogmatic spirit. We may come nearer the truth if we think of the love of God, rather than metaphysical attributes, as being embodied in Him.

In a time of crisis, we should remember that often men who are disenchanted with the church are attracted to Jesus Christ. He is often a good point of contact with men who live outside the church. If we are faithful to proclaim Him and are able to lead the church to take His claims over its life seriously, not only will men be redeemed but the church itself may be saved.

3 / MAKING THE GOSPEL PERSONAL

THE PULPIT HAS LOST POWER IN OUR TIME. THE VOICE OF THE preacher does not carry as far as it once did, nor does his message have the authority it once had. Yet, I am among those who believe that preaching is of crucial importance.

". . . Christ sent me not to baptize," Paul said, "but to preach the gospel" (I Cor. 1:17). I have the same feeling of urgency about preaching. I believe preaching is so vital that neither the preacher nor those who hear him can really live without the truths that preaching proclaims. In a day when much is being said about church renewal, I am sure that the church will not be revitalized unless the pulpit is renewed.

That which can renew the pulpit more than anything else is the preacher who occupies it. Yet, preaching cannot be dynamic unless the gospel has become personal in the life of the preacher. Paul could speak of "my gospel" (Rom. 2:16). He did not mean, however, that he possessed the gospel. The very opposite was true. The gospel possessed him. This was Paul's way of identifying with the gospel. The gospel was something that had happened to him. It had transformed his life, giving him a radically new direction.

How can the gospel be personal in the life of the preacher, becoming a creative spring of vitality and power for his preaching?

Believe the Gospel

The preacher has to believe the gospel. In believing he does not turn from his own emptiness to the vacuity of something else.

He turns from his own weakness to reality—the greatest of all realities: God's gracious action in Jesus Christ.

His faith is not that of a philosopher, detached from life, who carefully weighs the evidence for and against God, and finally concludes that the balances tilt in favor of God. He does more than climb a logical stairway of ideas. Faith is not giving intellectual assent to propositional truths. Faith is more than flashes of intuitional insight and mystical experience too ineffable for words. Faith is an act of the will. It is encounter and meeting. It is trust and commitment.

His trust is full and without reserve. He commits his life to Jesus Christ completely and trusts Him alone for his redemption. He is like a drowning man taking hold of a rope that has been thrown by a friend. He is like a pilot trusting his parachute after his plane has been shot down from beneath him. He is like a sailor leaving his torpedoed ship and getting into a life boat. He leaps from his own broken and inadequate life only to have his feet land on solid reality.

Experience the Gospel

Faith as encounter and trust allows the preacher to experience the gospel, to be able to say "my gospel." Yet, this is not to reduce the gospel to feeling and subjective experience. When this is done, we get a caricature of the gospel and it is preached in all kinds of broken and distorted forms. The preacher must let his subjective experience be tested by the Bible, the faith of the church, and the critical judgment of others.

The gospel has its source in happenings and events for which the preacher is not responsible in any way at all. He preaches about realities that are objective—just as objective as a mountain range. They are out there, and how the preacher feels about them does not change their validity. Yet, because the gospel is addressed to men in their deepest needs and most basic relationships, it can be experienced. That which is beyond and objective to the preacher can become within him grace, forgiveness, and power.

Here is the answer, in part, to the problem of authority in the pulpit: the preacher can speak with authority when objective truth has become subjective reality. What he says is compelling. The hearers do not pursue the academic questions of relatives and absolutes. They know that they are being confronted with reality that lays claim to their lives. It is a vital living authority.

When a preacher is a mere onlooker of God's saving events, which may be far removed in time and place, or a handler of speculative ideas, his preaching may have a kind of authority, but it will be cold, abstract, and lifeless. If he is a scholar, his authority will be pedantic and tedious. On the other hand, if the preacher's basic trust is in feelings, his authority will be as insubstantial as moods, and he will be open to all kinds of excesses and distortions. Rather than being sustained by the great historical stream of faith, his authority will be like foam upon the waters. It is only as that which God has done in history is done in him that the preacher can speak with living authority.

Our basic concern here, however, is with experiencing the gospel, and we have one of our finest examples in Paul.

When Paul became a Christian, he didn't change gods. The God of his fathers was the God of his Lord and Saviour Jesus Christ. Yet, the heart of his faith lay not in speculation about God nor in the mere recounting of God's saving action, but in an experience which was a meeting of the living God in Jesus Christ.

Paul's two great doctrines of salvation by grace and justification by faith were not born of intellectual reflection while he relaxed in an easy chair. They were born while he was on his face in the dust along a wayside. His spiritual pride had made him a harsh and injurious man, and he had persecuted the church of Jesus Christ. But wonder of all wonders, Christ forgave him and accepted him in pure grace. And Christ made only one demand: that he trust and believe. In simple trust, he found the answer to his most difficult religious question: How does an unrighteous man stand justified before a righteous God? The answer was almost too good to be true: not by moral striving or religious discipline but by faith. In the acceptance of God's grace in Christ, Paul's tormented life found peace, and his restless religious striving relaxed in the surrender of trust.

Paul's theology was an experience before it was a system of thought. Yet, Paul never decried the honest effort of the mind to express faith in as rational a way as possible. He brought the gifts of his own fine mind to his transforming experience in an effort to make his faith as intelligible and convincing as possible to others.

John Wesley, like Paul, knew what it was to experience the gospel. He has given us a very vivid account of that experience:

"In the evening I went unwillingly to a society in Aldersgate Street, where one was reading Luther's Preface to the Epistle of Romans. About a quarter before nine, while he was describing the change which God works in the heart through faith in Christ, I felt my heart strangely warmed. I felt I did trust in Christ alone, for my salvation; and an assurance was given me that He had taken away my sins, even mine, and saved me from the law of sin and death." Before that, Wesley had had an intellectual grasp of the gospel. But his preaching was as lifeless and sterile as desert sand. After his experience, his preaching had the power of tumbling waterfalls.

The late Bishop Angus Dun was a man who learned from his experience that only the love of God can redeem human tragedy. That was the heart of the gospel he preached. He was a man born to tragedy. He had a congenital defect that warped his limbs, which he overcame as a child. Later he lost a leg to polio. He once said: "I have learned that human experience is essentially tragic. It is only the love of God that redeems human tragedy."[1]

But there are two warnings for the preacher at this point. He must not demand that his experience be like that of Paul, Wesley, or Angus Dun. God will grant him an experience in keeping with his own needs and personality. The experience must be his own, rather than that of somebody else, before it can be authentic.

The second warning is this: The preacher must not expect to be carried constantly on the crest of a vital experience. He is human, and to be human is to go through dry seasons of the spirit. There may be long periods when God seems silent and far away. But he will be refreshed by remembering better days, when God was near and His word was clear. And he will keep looking up in hope. He will be like a farmer, during a long draught when his crops are withering, scanning the heavens for signs of rain, believing it will come before it is too late.

Preach the Gospel as Experienced

We are not to preach theoretical and abstract truths. And we are to do more than tell of events far removed, although our gospel is grounded in history. We are to speak of truth that is specific and concrete, of reality that has been enlivened by our own experience. While preaching about events from the past, we must transpose

---

1. *Time*, August 23, 1971, p. 39

them into the living present. In short, we are to preach the gospel we have experienced.

John, in his Gospel, points us in the direction of preaching the gospel as we have experienced it. This is one of the main emphases of his Gospel. Jesus, in response to two men who sought His dwelling place, responded, "Come and see" (John 1:39). It was an invitation to see and experience. One of the two men who questioned Jesus was Andrew, who found his brother Simon Peter and said to him, "We have found the Messiah, which is, being interpreted, the Christ" (John 1:41). Jesus, in talking to Nicodemus, a very intellectual and sophisticated man, said, "We speak that we do know, and testify that we have seen" (John 3:11). The Samaritan woman left her water pots at Jacob's well, went back up the hill where she found men loitering in the streets, and said to them: "Come, see a man, who told me all things that I ever did" (John 4:29, rsv). And the men, in response to her invitation, came down the hill and met Jesus, and then said to the woman: "It is no longer because of your words that we believe, for we have heard for ourselves, and we know that this is indeed the Savior of the world" (John 4:42, rsv). The man blind from his birth whom Jesus healed, when pressed to praise God, rather than Jesus, for his healing, responded: "Whether he is a sinner or no, I know not: one thing I know, that, whereas I was blind, now I see" (John 9:25). When on trial for his life before Pilate, Jesus asked Pilate after the Governor had inquired if He were King of the Jews, "Do you say this of your own accord, or did others say it to you about me?" (John 18:34, rsv). On the evening of the Resurrection, Thomas is presented as a skeptical man, demanding that he see the print of the nails in the hands of Jesus and the wounds in His side, before he would believe (John 20:25). A week later he had his demand granted. This incident, in its own odd way, is an extension of the theme: You bear witness to that which you have experienced.

The modern preacher can do no better than hear John. If he will, he can do two things: make great affirmations of faith, and preach, as already suggested, with a living authority.

As a freshman in college, I was burdened by guilt and conflict. Like Jacob of old, I wrestled with my problem one day far into the night. I told Christ I would not let Him go until he had blessed me. And Christ blessed me greatly when I made an unconditional surrender of my life to Him. His love overflowed my life, cleansing my heart of hatred and guilt and giving me a deep peace and an irresistible joy. That was the greatest and most real experience I have ever had. Since then, I have had many doubts, but they have made shipwreck of themselves on the reality of that experience. And when my preaching has power, it is infused with the spirit of that great hour or with experiences less dramatic but very real.

Live the Gospel

When God got ready to disclose Himself with finality, he took upon Himself our frail and fragile form. That was the Incarnation, and there was an absoluteness and once-for-allness about it. The Incarnation will never happen again. Yet, incarnation in a more relative and limited sense must continue.

There is a very real sense in which the gospel must be incarnate in the preacher. He must give hands and feet, lips and voice, breath and life to the gospel he is called to preach. He must embody the gospel. He must relate to people the way Jesus did. He must love them, accept them, serve them, give them dignity, and share their pain. Unless the gospel becomes incarnate in him, his preaching will be robbed of much of its power and effectiveness.

Fortunately the validity of the gospel does not depend upon the integrity of the preacher. It is validated by the integrity of Jesus Christ. Yet, the gospel is much more effective when preached from a pure heart and clean lips. When a preacher denies with his own life the love, grace, and forgiveness of the gospel he preaches, he does great damage to his message. Richard Baxter once said: "One proud, surly, lordly word, one needless contention, one covetous action, may cut the throat of many a sermon, and blast the fruit of all that you have been doing."[2]

St. Francis of Assisi one day said to several of his followers, "Let us go to the village over the way and preach." As they went, they met a humble pedestrian who was greatly burdened. Francis was in no hurry and listened carefully to his tale of woe. When the village was reached, Francis talked with the shopkeepers, spent time with the farmers at their fruit and vegetable stalls, and played with the children in the streets. On the way back they met a farmer with a load of hay, and Francis spent time with him. The morning gone, the group reached the monastery from where they had set out

2. Richard Baxter, *The Reformed Pastor* (Richmond: John Knox Press, 1963), p. 33

in the early morning. One of the followers, who was greatly disappointed, said to Francis, "Brother Francis, you said you were going to preach. The morning is spent and no sermon has been given." And the saintly Francis replied, "But we have been preaching all the way." Just so with the preacher who lives the gospel. Rather than having one pulpit, he has hundreds of them. He preaches all the way.

Despite the fact that preaching has lost prestige in our time, we do not lose heart. Having made the gospel our own and found in it a spring of new life, we keep on preaching. Ears not attuned to preaching may listen again. We may be supported by a great truth expressed by W. E. Sangster: "On his way to preach the gospel the most modest man may whisper to himself: 'nothing more important will happen in this town this week than the work I am now doing.' "[3] Preaching is still mighty important. Never doubt it.

3. W. E. Sangster, *Power in Preaching* (Nashville: Abingdon Press, 1958), p. 21

4 / THE PERSONAL CROSS IN PREACHING

I HEARD A GIFTED PREACHER A FEW SUMMERS AGO AT A PASTORS' conference. He was a preacher's preacher. He was obviously a craftsman in his study. He knew how to put his sermon together, and he was an artist in the pulpit. He preached with skill and finesse. His preaching was Biblically grounded. He was aware of current theological trends, and he was obviously sincere. Yet, there was something missing. He didn't grip us. Someone with insight remarked: "His answers are too easy. Everything is too pat. I don't sense pain and agony in his preaching."

The first thing I listen for in a preacher is not theology, his scholarship, or his eloquence. I listen for pain. Is there a personal cross in his preaching? Has he been too sheltered to know the agony of his world? Or has he exposed himself to the brokenness and hurt of his world so that he knows and experiences its pain? Are his words too glib and easy or have they been chastened by suffering? Has his faith been refined by agony and have his manners been made gentle by pain?

Not Pathological Pain

I am not speaking of pathological pain. The preacher, however, may be emotionally and spiritually sick. When this is the case, pathological pain often has its source in unresolved guilt. The guilt may be psychological, such as repressed hostilities against his parents of early years. A counselor or psychiatrist can help him with this. But the guilt may be real, resulting from breaking God's laws and injuring his fellows. The counselor and psychiatrist have severe limitations in helping him here. Like any common sinner, he must repent and trust the grace of God in Jesus Christ. And he must make restitution, if possible, to those he has hurt and injured.

The preacher with unresolved guilt may inflict pain on himself in an effort to atone for his sin. Preaching is not a joyous experience. It is not announcing good news essentially for him or anyone else. It is a painful and agonizing experience. He tortures and injures himself as an answer to his guilt.

Out of this unresolved guilt a preacher may develop an unhealthy martyr's complex. He may unconsciously seek pain from his own hands or the hands of others. He may enjoy his own severity, and he may enjoy the criticism and rejection of his people. He may create situations that will produce tension and conflict.

Paul was aware of a false kind of martyrdom. ". . . if I deliver my body to be burned," he said, "but have not love, I gain nothing" (I Cor. 13:3, RSV). Only love that makes life expendable for something greater than itself can be healthy and creative.

But the preacher may handle his guilt in another unhealthy way. He may project it onto his people. Therefore he makes them suffer. Preaching that inflicts suffering on the congregation may be effective for a time, appealing to his ego and vanity as well as giving him some relief vicariously. Many of his congregation, having unresolved guilt, may enjoy pain inflicted by his preaching. Their suffering seems to atone for their sins and offer some release from their guilt. But a reaction sets in, sooner or later, against this kind of preaching. It affords at best a sporadic and false release from guilt. Rather than a healthy release from guilt, the final end is heaping guilt upon guilt.

The preacher suffering from this kind of pathological pain develops a certain pattern of preaching. This happens whether he makes himself or his congregation the object of suffering. His preaching is moralistic. Christ is another Moses, more austere than the first one, and Christ gives a new law more severe than the old. God is seen as a severe judge. He forgets that law came through Moses but that grace and truth came through Jesus Christ. He does not know that God is more like a loving Father welcoming home the prodigal from a far country than a heartless judge. He forgets that the essence of the highest and most elaborate code of law is fulfilled in the law of love. The gospel is, for him, more like bad news than good news.

The Personal Cross as Authentic Pain

Jesus, on the first Easter evening, appeared suddenly in the midst of His frightened disciples who were behind locked doors. He greeted them in a familiar manner: " . . . Peace be unto you. When he had so said," John tells us, "he showed unto them his hands and his side . . ." (John 20:20, 21). Jesus identified Himself in terms of the marks of His suffering. He showed his disciples His hands, which carried the marks of Roman nails, and His side, with the wounds put there by a Roman sword.

Marks of authentic pain should identify the modern preacher. Authentic pain is his personal cross. Such pain is created by sensitivity, involvement, identification, and exposure to reality. It represents health while pathological pain is the result of sickness.

Three types of authentic pain should be felt in the preacher's life.

1. *The Cross of Doubt.* Doubt is one of the characteristics of our age. Many of the landmarks of faith have been swept away, and many people find it hard to believe. Others hold on to faith but demand that the traditional faith be recast into new thought forms, having greater relevance. The generation preceding us had fewer questions and more answers. Our generation has more questions and fewer answers. The doubt of our age has its own peculiar pain.

Our age is experiencing one of the sporadic moods of the Bible. "How long wilt thou forget me, O Lord?", asked the psalmist, "forever? how long wilt thou hide thy face from me?" (Ps. 13:1). And Isaiah, caught up in the same kind of mood, could say: "Verily thou art a God that hideth thyself . . ."(Isa. 45:15). Modern man often feels that God has abandoned him. God is like a skipper who has forsaken his ship with its crew and passengers, leaving them to manage the best they can upon the high seas.

William Hamilton has written: "Little wonder that Lent is the only season when we are at home, and the cry of dereliction from the cross is the only biblical word that can speak to us. If Jesus can wonder about being forsaken by God, are we to be blamed if we wonder."[1] Many people feel that way in our time.

---

1. William Hamilton, *The New Essence of Christianity* (New York: Association Press, 1961), p. 58

The preacher, refusing to live a sheltered life and exposing himself to his world, must feel its doubt with its pain. Not to feel this pain means he has insulated himself from a kind of reality that marks his world. He may have once suffered from this kind of doubt but, having worked through to a positive faith, he will never forget its pain.

P. T. Forsyth, more than a half century ago, wrote one of the really great books on preaching: *Positive Preaching and the Modern Mind.* It is being widely used in our day. "We must all preach to our age," he said, "but woe to us if it is our age we preach, and only hold up the mirror to the time. . . . Preach to Isben's world, and there are few that you will miss. Only do not preach his word."[2]

This is a wise word to the modern preacher. He must preach to his age, which means he must address an age of doubt. But he must be much more than an echo of that doubt. His voice, without being dogmatic, must be a firm voice of faith. Few things will so bridge the gap between him and many who hear him as for his congregation to sense in him the pain of doubt which they experience.

The preacher who knows the pain of doubt will not reject men who find it hard to believe. He will accept them without being judgmental. He will relate to them the way Jesus did to the father of an epileptic boy whose life was pulled between faith and doubt. Jesus did not rebuke him for his doubt. He accepted him as he was and said: "If you can! All things are possible to him who believes." And feeling secure in Jesus' acceptance, the father made a hopeful response: "I believe; help my unbelief" (Mark 9:23, 24, RSV). And today a man of doubt who experiences such full acceptance by a preacher may find the strength that enables him to believe.

2. *The Cross of Aloneness.* There is a beautiful story in Exodus about Moses receiving strength when weary in battle. As long as Moses held up his hands, he and his men won against the Amalekites. But he grew so tired that he could no longer hold up his hands. So ". . . Aaron and Hur held up his hands, one on one side, and the other on the other side; so his hands were steady until the going down of the sun" (Exod. 17:12, RSV).

But all battles are not fought on battlefields. Often a battle is fought in a man's soul. There you are away from hands that sup-

---

2. P. T. Forsyth, *Positive Preaching and the Modern Mind* (Grand Rapids: Wm. B. Eerdmans Publishing Co., 1964), p. 152

port you and voices that comfort you. You struggle in the aloneness of your soul. And often terrible pain is involved.

Jacob, upon returning home after twenty years to face a hostile brother who had threatened his life, sent his family across the brook Jabbok, but he himself stayed behind alone. "And Jacob was left alone; and a man wrestled with him until the breaking of the day!" (Gen. 32:24, RSV). Moses had to leave the people at the base of Mt. Sinai and go up into the mountain alone to meet God. Jesus took with Him Peter, James, and John into the Garden of Gethsemane on that dark night of His soul. But the solitariness of his decision drew Him a little way beyond His disciples. There, alone, upon his face, with sweat like drops of blood falling to the ground, he prayed: "Father, if thou art willing, remove this cup from me; nevertheless not my will, but thine, be done" (Luke 22: 42, RSV).

The preacher cannot escape the pain of solitariness. He must know those lonely heights of decision. He must go down into those deep valleys where he wrestles with dark forces that would silence his prophetic voice and turn him from paths in which a true servant of God must walk. No one can accompany him to those heights nor descend with him into those depths. He must go alone.

A great decision the preacher has to make is whether he will preach the word the people want to hear or preach the word God calls upon him to speak. The decision he makes will have a significant bearing on whether he is popular or unpopular, secure or insecure, successful or unsuccessful as judged by popular standards, accepted or rejected. Preachers of every age have to make this decision. Those of the first generation affirmed, "We must obey God rather than men" (Acts 5:29, RSV). But the question for the modern preacher is particularly crucial since the church of today has been so culture-ridden. Too often the church has demanded a message that reflected the spirit and values of the culture more than the gospel of Jesus Christ. Now that the church is seeking to free itself from cultural bondage, there is a large segment of the church which is defensive. Especially is there strong resistance to the social dimension of the gospel from this group. Many preachers, who have chosen to speak the word of God rather than the word of the culture, are very insecure. Often they lose their pulpits. Men are driven to those lonely heights and forced to their knees as they make the decision to be prophetic.

Phillips Brooks has spoken forcefully to us concerning this matter: "The timid minister is as bad as the timid surgeon. Courage is good everywhere, but it is necessary here. If you are afraid of men and a slave to their opinion, go and do something else. Go and make shoes to fit them. Go even and paint pictures which you know are bad, but which suit their bad taste. But do not keep on all your life preaching sermons which shall not say what God sent you to declare, but what they hire you to say. Be courageous. Be independent."[3]

3. *The Cross of Identification.* Christianity is a religion of incarnation. "The Word became flesh and dwelt among us . . ." (John 1:14, RSV). God in Jesus Christ took upon Himself our life, with all its pain and weakness. The Incarnate Son of God became the Suffering Servant. He washed the dirty feet of men like us and He suffered with and for us men.

As has already been suggested, there was a once-for-allness, an absoluteness, about the Incarnation of Jesus Christ. It will never happen again. Yet, the preacher must incarnate an accepting and healing love which enables him to identify with men in their weakness and suffering. The identification will not be as full and complete as was the identification effected by Jesus Christ but it must be real.

Job said: "I was eyes to the blind and feet to the lame" (Job 29:15, RSV). Ezekiel told of coming to his own people who were dispirited captives far from home, ". . . I sat where they sat," he said, "and remained there astonished among them for seven days" (Ezek. 3:15). One wonders if a man can preach with real power and effectiveness unless he has known this kind of identification.

Not only does great preaching come from this kind of identification. Great prayer, as well, comes from it. Possibly the greatest prayer of intercession was given by Moses after he descended from Mt. Sinai to find his people so soon returned to idolatry. "Alas, this people have sinned a great sin; they have made for themselves gods of gold. But now, if thou wilt forgive their sin—and if not, blot me, I pray thee out of thy book which thou hast written" (Exod. 32:31-32, RSV). These were his people and he was involved in their life. If they could not be forgiven and saved, he did not want to be spared their tragedy.

---

3. Phillips Brooks, *Eight Lectures on Preaching* (London: S.P.C.K., Holy Trinity Church, 1959), p. 59

The preacher must be able to feel the joy and fright of little children, and he must share with youth their idealism and frustration. He must feel the strain and tension of young married couples getting established in homes and businesses, and he must know the responsibilities of adults in middle years who carry heavy burdens in the heat of the day. He must identify with old people from whom the years have taken much as they face the sunset of life. He must be with all kinds of people across the wide spectrum of life, sharing their hopes and fears, successes and failures, health and sickness, faith and doubts.

Dick Sheppard was such a preacher. Plagued with illness and offering the asthmatics' prayer, "Give us this day our daily breath," he carried a personal cross which was heavier than his asthma. Yet, he gave himself unsparingly to his people. Frequently he would sit up all night with a sick parishioner. When he was dean of Canterbury he would get up at six-thirty in the morning to meet the cathedral workers as they began their day's work. He loved people and whatever concerned them was his concern. He was never a stranger to their pain. When he died, an East London dock worker said: "Good Gawd, mother, what shall we do without 'im?" And when people heard the sad news, they found themselves saying, not how fond they were of him but how much he cared for them. Robert J. McCracken has said of this man: "There is no doubt at all that this fellow-feeling, this self-identification with human need, was the strength of his preaching and the secret of his hold on people."[4]

Wherever Christianity is carried its best known symbol is a cross. The cross will not let us forget that Jesus Christ was wounded for our transgressions and that with His stripes we are healed. The preacher who knows a personal cross is best able to tell his world where it can be healed.

---

4. Robert J. McCracken, *The Making of the Sermon* (New York: Harper and Brothers, 1956), p. 20

5 / PREACHING WHERE PEOPLE ARE

ONE OF THE CHARGES MADE AGAINST THE PULPIT IS THAT IT IS irrelevant. Laymen especially see this as a part of the pulpit crisis of our time. They say frequently that the preacher answers questions they do not ask, preaches about abstract truths while they wrestle with concrete problems, talks about spiritual reality that seems far removed from the earthy and mundane settings of their lives, and uses language that is difficult to understand.

In the Incarnation, God came to where people were. The preacher must seek nothing less than this for his sermon. He must preach where people are.

The Two Poles of Preaching

The two poles of preaching are God's redemptive action and people. God's saving action redeems people, and it must be people to whom the gospel is addressed.

James T. Cleland speaks of the bifocal nature of preaching. "The Word of God is bifocal," he writes. "It has its head in the heavens, but its feet are on the ground."[1] In order to stress the two poles of preaching, Cleland likens it to an ellipse. "A sermon is not a circle but an ellipse. It does not have a single focus but two focuses. It is not a case of being Bible centered, or man centered. It is the conscious careful recognition of both the historic faith and the folk in front of the pulpit. There are always two centers of interest in a sound sermon—the historic faith and the present day.

---

1. James T. Cleland, *Preaching to be Understood* (Nashville: Abingdon Press, 1965), p. 45

Which is more important? The answer is: What focus is more important in drawing an ellipse? Both are indispensable. Together they form the word of God."[2]

Both poles must be held together in a careful balance. God's redemptive action makes preaching authentic, while awareness of and concern for people make preaching relevant. Some preachers, in an attempt to be authentic, fail to be relevant and lose their hearers. While other preachers, in seeking to be relevant and contemporary, fail to be authentic and lose the Word of God. The loss of either makes preaching ineffective.

Where People Always Are

The preacher, in an attempt to be contemporary and up to the minute, may overlook two important facts. First, in the midst of the shifting scenes with their changing moods, new values, and novel interest, men keep a permanent stance. There are great hopes, concerns, and problems that do not change with the times. They are as constant as human nature. The preacher must not forget this, lest he become like the ancient Athenians who "spent their time in nothing except telling or hearing something new" (Acts 17:21, RSV). He can find himself addressing volatile moods rather than speaking to the great hopes and deep tragedy in human life.

Second, the authentic gospel has a kind of built-in relevance. God's revelation is a self-disclosure to people. God's Word is thrust at the heart of human existence, both individual and corporate, where there are hope and despair, good and evil, and almost infinite possibilities of tragedy.

As already suggested in an earlier chapter, Paul thought of the gospel as a kind of ellipse with the death and resurrection of Jesus Christ as being the two foci. Here is the gospel's answer to the two great tragedies of human existence, sin and death. Man is a sinner and man dies. Therefore, when a preacher preaches about the cross and resurrection in their truly Biblical sense, he cannot fail to be relevant. Men stand always, everywhere under the shadow of sin and death.

Dietrich Ritschl has spoken of the built-in relevance of the gospel. "The desperation concerning 'communication' in homiletical literature and in discussion among preachers indicates very clearly that the Word of God is wrongly conceived as a religious

---

2. Ibid., pp. 42-43

word, which one has to make relevant, as if it were not the word itself that makes itself relevant. Thus Paul M. Van Buren writes, in an excellent article on preaching. 'God's Word is life itself. For a world that lies in death, the Word is the resurrection and the life. There can be no question of our making the Word relevant to the world. . . .' The Word of God is far more relevant than we could ever be, and if we will be obedient to the Bible, truly obedient, then we shall find ourselves far more deeply involved in the lives of our people and in situation than we ever were when we were anxious to be relevant".[3]

While I feel that Ritschl has overstated his case, we would do well to heed his warning.

Kyle Haselden has shared the same concern: "The fundamental question about the relevancy of our preaching has to do with its genuineness rather than with its contemporaneity. Does it deal with the essential stuff of human nature and the human experience? Are there sounds in it that are as primitive and as elemental as a baby's cry, food in it as basic as bread, vistas in it which open the way to God's throne?"[4]

Where People Are Now

While I have emphasized the permanent stance of people, I do not minimize the contemporary situation. That is important, too. The gospel must be addressed to people where they are now. If you are not aware of their current interests, you may miss them, and, therefore, not have the opportunity to speak to their more permanent needs. Their present concerns, though shifting and changing, may be the door to the real center of their lives.

Phillips Brooks wrote of how untimely a sermon is "if it deals only with the abstractions of eternity, and has no word to help men who are dizzied with the whirl and blinded with the darkness of today."[5]

Helmut Thielicke has stressed the importance of making the sermon contemporary. "The sermon must be contemporary. It must correspond with the time in which it is preached."[6] And

---

3. Dietrich Ritschl, *A Theology of Proclamation* (Richmond: John Knox Press, 1963), p. 50
4. Op. cit., p. 39
5. Op. cit., p. 141
6. Helmut Thielicke, *The Trouble with the Church* (New York: Harper and Row, 1965), p. 97

David James Randolph has emphasized the same truth. "A ser-mon," he writes, "is an address to a particular people at a particu-lar time in a particular place. . . . It is a turning point in preaching when the preacher begins to preach to faces, to particular persons and problems, seen against the landscape of modernity."[7]

The preacher must be aware of at least three things in address-ing the gospel to where people are now.

First, he must preach the redemptive action of God in terms of the experience and language of his people.

God's spokesmen in the Bible did this. They didn't appeal to abstract and ethereal experience. They spoke to people where they stood historically with their political, social, economic and spiritual involvements. And they eschewed an esoteric and technical lan-guage. There was the ring of life and vitality in their words. When God spoke His final word through His Son, He did the same thing. Jesus Christ spoke our language, set His feet in all our dusty ways, underwent our pain and temptation, and suffered our death. The setting of His life was historical and concrete.

Since language is born of experience, the two must be held together. If I appeal to unknown and abstract experience through familiar language, or speak of familiar experience through difficult and technical language, I miss my people. I fail to speak to them where they are now.

Second, the preacher must give universal truth a particular application.

The Bible appeals to truth and reality that men experience everywhere and at all times. It is universal. The Bible speaks of day and night, light and darkness, earth and sky; sleeping and waking, work and rest, withdrawal from and return to the busy world, strength and weakness, sickness and health, life and death; laughter and weeping, hope and despair, love and hate; right and wrong, friendship and enmity, alienation and reconciliation; the common-place and mystery, faith and doubt, man and God.

Yet, the universal truth is given a much more immediate, limited, and provincial application. Metaphors and symbols lifted from limited, geographical settings become the vehicles of this truth. The Bible speaks of vineyards, olive trees, pomegranates, figs, wheat, barley, dry seasons, rainy seasons, shepherds, and sheep. The

7. David James Randolph, *The Renewal of Preaching* (Philadelphia: For-tress, 1969), pp. 44-45

Old Testament speaks basically to a special people, limited by their geography and history. It is aware of their peculiar experiences: their particular history, their feeling that they were the chosen of God, sense of mission and destiny, special gifts, and God's redemptive action in the midst of their lives.

In the New Testament, the focus is on a particular person as well as a particular people. Jesus Christ, the particular person, spoke of God's love and redemption for all men. Yet, His life was historical and dated. He was a child of His time, and His speech and thought patterns had the coloring of a particular place, time, and history. The church, the particular people, is set within history and, while not limited by geographical, national, social, or racial boundaries, has the stamp of its particular time and place upon its life.

The modern preacher must remember that truth is sharpest and most pungent when a universal need is focused and concentrated in terms of a more limited experience. The universal need for justice, for example, is most demanding when felt in the life of a particular community.

The pastor must keep in mind his church, set against the background of a particular community with a special history. The church I serve is in Martinsville, Virginia, a city of 20,000 located in southside Virginia. We are a rapidly growing industrial town, with economic vitality and confidence in our future. Yet, we suffer from racial tension, and we are going through the painful transition from a typical Southern town to a more cosmopolitan community. Many of the social problems that run the full spectrum of our culture are thrown into focus here. Our church is the oldest Baptist church in our city, and draws most of its members from the middle class. I must address the gospel to the particular mentality and experience of our people. If I do not, the gospel will not have the relevance and cutting edge it should.

Third, the modern preacher must be aware of the pervading mentality of the time.

I feel the modern mind can be characterized as a secular mind, a mind tempered by revolution, and a mind that is both hopeful and afraid.

The secular mind is a this worldly mind, locked in a time-space dimension. It does not look for reality beyond man, his world, and his history. It does not see life set against the background of an

eternal dimension. It exalts science and tangible values. It is human-
istic, putting trust in man, finding the ultimate in human values.
More and more the universe is seen as being bounded by man's
mind rather than being transcended by God. There is a loss of
religious faith. This is a mind that doubts.

Can the gospel speak of this kind of mind? Yes, it has definite
points of contact with it.

Space and time have their validity. They are God's orders and
He has pronounced them good. Man has great value, and human
values are to take precedence over all other values. And science
has its significant role. Upon creating man, God instructed him to
subdue the earth and science is man's instrument of mastery.

It is also important to remember that the Bible sees God's saving
events as not taking place essentially within religious institutions
and by altars presided over by priests, but occurring out in the vast
secular world. The prophets were able to see both God's judgment and mercy beyond ecclesiastical walls. God was doing something out there in the world.

The modern preacher, if he is a prophet, will look out upon his
world to see what God is doing there. He will not make the mistake
of believing that God acts only on Sunday, during an hour of worship, and in sacred places. God is not the prisoner of sacred buildings, holy hours, and religious ceremonies. He will look for God in
our world with its war and striving after peace, the emergence of
backward peoples with their new sense of dignity and destiny, the
rebellion of youth and the rise of counter cultures, the communication crisis, tensions that are sometime violent and efforts at reconciliation, poverty and wealth that stand in stark contrast, and
technology which is a growing confirmation that God has put all
things under man's feet. When God's judgment and mercy can be
traced there, people will know how inescapably relevant the gospel
is. Now, as in the Old and New Testaments, God's redemptive action
may have a secular setting.

Secularity has its severe limitations and the preacher must not
be blind to these. It has truth but not the whole truth. It tells only
a part of the story, but the part it tells is important. Here the
preacher can make contact with the secular mind.

The modern mind is also tempered by radical change.

We find ourselves in one of the great transitional periods of
history. We are in the midst of a revolution. Old structures are

being torn down, and new ones are being erected. Old landmarks are being swept away, and long respected institutions, are being dismantled. Our social, moral, intellectual, and spiritual life is being subjected to radical change. The modern revolution may be as deep and far reaching as the fall of the Roman Empire, the Renaissance, the Protestant Revolution, and the Industrial Revolution.

Can the gospel speak to a mind tempered by revolution? Yes, because the gospel is no stranger to revolution. When the gospel is authentically preached and faithfully lived radical change is sure to follow. We should not forget that the early apostles were described as men who "have turned the world upside down." (Acts 17:6)

There are basic ideas in Christianity that are revolutionary: that God takes history seriously as testified by the Incarnation; that history is dynamic rather than static; the claim that every life has worth and dignity; that no social order ever meets God's demand for justice.

The purpose of the gospel is neither to react negatively to the status quo nor to give religious sanction to it. The purpose is to bring men and women into a saving relationship with God through Jesus Christ and create social situations where people can become authentic persons with worth and dignity. When this happens, a new vitality is released, demanding new forms. The old wine skins can no longer hold the new wine. The status quo is changed under the impact of the gospel. This does not mean, however, that the gospel sanctions all forces at work in a time of revolution. Many of these it will have to oppose. But it does more than react negatively. It seeks to create new channels for a greater dignity, freedom, justice, and security.

The modern mind is both hopeful and frightened.

If the population explosion and the possibility of nuclear war can be controlled, we may see the time approaching when no child need cry himself to sleep at night because of hunger, no person need shiver in a threadbare garment, and no man need sleep without a roof over his head.

Modern education battles with success the problem of illiteracy. Medical science increasingly brings its blessings to men everywhere. There is a rising expectancy concerning physical, economic, medical and cultural values.

But what is of greater significance is a rising expectancy for human values. Never before have such words as freedom, dignity, and equality had such magical power over men the world over. The hearts of men everywhere leap up at their sound. We think of the new nations that have appeared at such an accelerated rate since World War II. Never before in history have so many been made so free in such a brief period of time to determine their destiny.

Yet, we are not so sure we can control the population explosion and nuclear war. There is the possibility that men will crowd themselves off their planet and the threat of nuclear war lies across their lives. And we are in trouble with our physical environment. The earth, made sick by our refuse and pollution, threatens to disgorge us.

Our gospel can speak to the paradoxical mood of the modern mind. It warns us against utopian hope since man is sinful. Yet, it can lift us from despair and give us hope since God has entered our history in Jesus Christ to save us.

Since the gospel is God's saving action directed to people, we must realize that the hour in the pulpit falls far short of its goal unless the gospel we preach is directed to people in their deepest needs where they are. We should put forth great effort in helping the time in the pulpit fulfill itself, so that, rather than being a dull interlude, it may truly become the greatest hour of the week.

6 / COMMUNICATING THE GOSPEL

PREACHING, BY ITS VERY NATURE, IS COMMUNICATION, AND YET THE pulpit is facing a communication crisis. The church is very conscious of this crisis. "Nowhere is the importance of the problem of communication more clearly understood than in the life of the church," writes Theodore O. Wedel. "Wherever the church's task of mission and evangelism is today being studied under a recognition of the church's minority status on our globe or its engagement in a confrontation with a world dedicating itself to secular idolatries, the problem of communication leaps to the forefront of attention. On the ecumenical scene few themes are more widely discussed than the question: How to communicate the gospel?"[1]

How do you communicate the gospel to a generation to whom the gospel often sounds strange and to a world that turns deaf ears? This question must be honestly and seriously faced.

Make Possible Non-Verbal Communication

The most effective communication is non-verbal. It takes place on a deep level of feeling and awareness. It is made possible by the preacher being an authentic person, speaking with urgency and authority.

It is especially important that the preacher of our time be an authentic person. He has been disrobed of former ecclesiastical prestige, and professional props are being knocked from beneath

1. Theodore O. Wedel, *The Gospel in a Strange New World* (Philadelphia: The Westminster Press, 1968), p. 23

him. He can no longer hide beneath his role. He must be a real person. He must stand on his own feet, integrity, and personhood. His people must feel in him the grace, love, acceptance, and forgiveness about which he preaches. His preaching will be grounded in Biblical truth, but it must also be an overflow from his life.

There must be urgency about his preaching. He is dealing with crucial issues, matters of life and death. What he says is important to his people. He is not coercive, manipulative, or intimidating, but you can't miss the direction in which he is moving. He is moving toward a decision. He will call for a commitment of life.

There must be authority about what he says. It will not be a tedious, pedantic, and dead authority. You feel that he is an ambassador, that he has been sent by somebody. He has a word he has been commissioned to speak and he must say it. Yet, that word has become his own. He does not mechanically parrot his message, but speaks truth that has found lodging at the center of his life.

Such authority was observed in F. L. Anderson, who came in his youth to be the pastor of the Second Baptist Church in Rochester, New York. After his first sermon, an elderly woman said to him: "How can you, young as you are, expect to please seven hundred people?" He gave the only answer a minister should be able to give to such a question, yet it was open to being misconstrued as pious and sanctimonious. "I did not come to please seven hundred people," he replied. "I came to please one." He knew whose he was and the truth that had been given him to speak. While always bold and courageous because he spoke with authority, he became the warm and beloved pastor of a great church.

Trust the Power of Words

While we live in a culture where visual communication is in ascendancy, we should not mistrust the power of the spoken word. We should not sell it short. It represents something deep and primordial in human life. There is great truth in the Biblical concept of the spoken word: Something of the person goes forth in the word he speaks. The word is a projection of the inner life of the person in a way the visual image cannot achieve. It comes from the source of thought, reflection, and feeling. It comes from the center of life.

D. W. Cleverly Ford has written of the indispensable use of the spoken word. "A man is a talking being. It is speech that distinguishes him from the other animals. Presumably the animals communicate with each other (there is evidence for this), but man needs more than communication; he needs communication of speech. Speech, then, is necessary for any life which is truly and fully human. Speech is also the most effective form of communication. The picture, the dance, the performance of instrumental music are also means of communication, but they are assisted by descriptions in words which both make the medium convey a meaning to more people, and sharpen and clarify what that meaning is, or may be. Visual aids, too, despite their increasingly widespread use today, are but aids to verbal communication, not replacements."[2]

It should be remembered that Biblical faith puts great trust in the spoken word. The religion of Israel was much more a matter of hearing than seeing. Israel, of all the ancient peoples, refused to represent their God visually. No man could see God and live. Israel was forbidden to make any graven image. Pictures and sculpture were not to be found in their sanctuaries. They were barren of visual imagery. Yet, great dependency was put on the spoken word. By the word of God the world was created and by his word his creation was sustained. The word of God came with overwhelming power upon the prophets. Amos Wilder has reminded us that "Jesus was a voice, not a penman, a herald not a scribe, a watchman with his call in the market-place and the temple."[3]

Yet, the preacher dare not be careless about how he uses words. If he is, he will rob verbal communication of much of its potential power. How he selects and uses words is of great importance.

Every discipline, including theology, has its technical language. Faith, like science, has its own language. It may be a handicap in a sense; if so, it is a handicap the preacher has to live with. Yet, he dare not use theological language in an exclusive sense. If he does, he will lose his congregation. His people will find his language abstract, unintelligible, and uninteresting. They will miss the truth he is seeking to convey. His theological language has to be enlivened, amplified, and made communicable. How will he do that? He has his best example in Jesus Christ. Jesus used analogies, drew parallels, told stories, and lifted experiences from the life about Him. The preacher must draw from modern life, define terms, use analogies, give illustrations, and touch theological terms with life.

2. Op. cit., p. 79-80
3. Op. cit., p. 21

To put it another way, one must use language that laymen can understand. Jesus talked about God in the language of shepherds, farmers, craftsmen, and merchants. Amos Wilder has written of Jesus' ability to talk about God in the language of laymen. "But he said the same thing in what we call layman's language in his parables of the Kingdom, parables of judgment, etc. What does this mean except that he brought theology down into daily life and into the immediate everyday situation? Here is a clue for the modern preacher, indeed for the Christian whatever his form of witness."[4]

Paul did the same thing. He spoke about God and the spiritual life in categories taken from the life about him and in language understood by the ordinary person. Justification, redemption, reconciliation, and adoption are now technical theological terms. But they were not when Paul used them. They were terms lifted from the common life about him. Justification came from the courts, redemption from slavery, reconciliation from the common experiences of estrangement in life, and adoption from the family and court.

The preacher should use words that have vigor, strength, and concreteness. Salvation has not come through abstract, universal truths. It has come through a person who was exceptionally vigorous and vital and who lived out His life in a concrete, historical setting. It takes such language to tell about Him.

Pulpit speech should be more than heavenly language. There should be a quality of earthiness about it. "The Word was made flesh and dwelt among us." How can you be more human and earthy than that? Jesus Christ has walked in our dusty ways. Language about Him can be too spiritual and rarefied. Speak of Him as He was.

Contemporize the Message

How do you preach the Word of God, spoken to ancient man, to modern man? An ancient book, unless its truth is contemporized, may have little more meaning than an ancient city. You may walk through the streets of an ancient city, now in ruins, and find it interesting, but it cannot help you with the problems of an urban culture. It may be interesting to vividly reconstruct historical situations of the Bible, breathe life into Biblical characters, and

4. Ibid., p. 94

trace God's dealing with them, but the congregation wants to know what God is saying and doing now in the midst of their lives. Unless the preacher can transpose the ancient reality into a modern setting, point to God's action in today's world, he and his congregation will be like ships that pass in the night. They do not make contact.

Take the characters of the Bible, disrobe them of their ancient garb, and dress them in modern business suits. Take them from their plodding pedestrian gait and put them behind the wheels of high-powered automobiles on modern highways. Lift them from donkeys and put them on jet planes. Remove them from their simple settings of life and put them in the complexities of the twentieth century. A wonderful thing will be discovered. They ask the basic questions we ask, and their answers can help guide us to find solutions to our problems. But we have to hear them ask those questions the way we ask them and we have to receive the Biblical answers in terms understandable to us.

A sermon, for example, may be given on the Good Samaritan. Tell it as Jesus did. Vividly reconstruct the historical situation. But you must go further. The story should be put in a modern setting. What if it should happen in Martinsville, Virginia, a city of 20,000 in the southside of the state. Who would be the victim of the way and how would he have been injured? Who would be the priest and Levite in this city? And who would be the Good Samaritan in this Southern culture? The story would then live, and God would be able to speak through it to the people where they are.

The Hebrew prophets saw the judgment of God in the invading armies from Egypt, Assyria, and Babylon, and Jesus saw it hovering over doomed Jerusalem. But what meaning does such judgment, so remote and far away, have for modern man? Where is God's judgment in today's world? Can the preacher show God's judgment in the racial violence of our time, rioting in our streets, the widening gap between the rich and the poor, and the deterioration of the inner city? Where is the healing, forgiving, and reconciling action of God today?

Preach Relational Truths

Biblical faith is expressed through relational realities. Its truth is given, not in abstract, universal principles, but in concrete, historical situations and persons, especially one Person, where truth is validated by broken relationships being healed. Men are urged, not to give intellectual assent to propositioned truths, but to enter into redemptive relationships with God and their fellows. So basic is this, that the Biblical revelation was given within a context of relationship. This was a covenant which is a unique relationship between God and His people. God was present and disclosed Himself in covenant relationship. The distinguishing thing about Israel was not that they were better or more spiritually sensitive than other people of the ancient world. As a matter of fact they were not. They were often spiritually dull and prone to evil. That which distinguished them was that they were a covenant people. Why God chose them was always a mystery. It was God's secret.

Jeremiah foresaw a new covenant that would be more inward and spiritual than the first one. "But this is the covenant which I will make with the house of Israel after those days, says the Lord: I will put my law within them, and I will write it upon their hearts; and I will be their God, and they shall be my people" (Jer. 31:33, RSV). Jesus fulfilled Jeremiah's vision when in the Upper Room He took wine, after He had blessed it and said: "This cup is the new covenant in my blood" (I Cor. 11:25, RSV). So fundamental is this covenant relationship that our Bible should be the Old and New Covenants rather than the Old and New Testaments.

The great Christian truths are relational in nature. Salvation is seen in terms of relationship. Persons are not saved in isolation. They are restored to God who is the source of their life. This is relationship in its deepest dimension. Faith is not giving intellectual assent to a body of theological dogmas but putting trust in a person, the Person of Jesus Christ. Justification is relational in nature: Men are declared to stand before God as just men, not because of their own goodness, but because of their faith in the grace and goodness of Jesus Christ. The same is true of the doctrine of reconciliation. Men who have been estranged from God and their fellows, are reconciled to God and their brothers through Jesus Christ. The church, in its basic nature, is relational. It is the fellowship of the reconciled, both to God and men, who have been given a mission of reconciliation. The Christian ethic has relationship as its fundamental quality. It is not code oriented, but person oriented in terms of love. We are to love our neighbors as ourselves. Love is the fulfilling of the law.

Modern man, like all his forefathers, finds his life fulfilled in terms of relationship. Yet his life is uprooted and mobile, with a growing sense of anonymity. He finds strong, permanent relationships hard to establish. His heart cries out for relationship although it is often a muffled cry. Couch the gospel, not in terms of sterile dogma, but living relationships and he will hear you. Express theological truth in terms of relationship with God and neighbor, where both judgment and grace are present, and you can communicate with him.

Preach Dialogically

There is a reaction against authoritarian preaching in our time. Preaching today must be dialogical, which means that there must be an interchange between the pulpit and pew. Preaching is no longer one-directional. It must be two directional.

Reuel L. Howe warns against what he calls the "monological illusion." It is a kind of communication that tells people what they ought to know. He believes the monological discourse from the pulpit is at an end. There must be encounter, engagement, interchange, and dialogue in preaching.

This may be achieved in formal ways. Dialogue may follow the sermon, or there may be a sharing of thinking with laymen in preparing the sermon. Laymen may give a critique of the sermon on tape, and the pastor may then listen to the tape to see how well he has communicated the truth. But dialogue may occur less formally.

The pastor may know his people so well and be so closely identified with them that he senses such responses as these going on in the minds of the worshipers as they hear the sermon: "That answers my question"; "He is speaking to me"; "That is new light on the truth"; "I do not agree"; "I must give more thought to that." That is dialogical preaching.

A preacher may reject dialogical preaching because preaching is proclamation. He is like a herald announcing good news. We should never forget that this is the essential nature of preaching, and, when it ceases to be proclamation, it ceases to be preaching. Yet, the hearers have the right to ask the herald to amplify the meaning of the good news, show why it is good news for them, and what responses they should make to it. When this happens, dialogue occurs.

The theological basis for dialogical preaching is the Incarnation where God made a full identification with us men. God got inside the human situation and spoke in human words so there could be a truly human response. It was not an overwhelming word but a word that elicited the responses of men. It was dialogical.

Communicating the gospel is no easy task in our time. It will challenge the best ability of the preacher. Yet, it is not an impossible task. It can be done. And the preacher must realize that the people to whom he preaches have deep needs that only the gospel of Jesus Christ can satisfy. The knowledge of this will be a powerful incentive for putting forth his best effort in achieving this communication.

7 / LETTING THE SERMON BE EMPOWERED

PREACHING MAY BECOME BURDENSOME, LEAVING THE PREACHER depressed and exhausted. This is sure to happen when the preacher takes himself too seriously, feeling that he is responsible for giving power to the sermon. The truth is that sources of power in preaching lie essentially, not within the preacher, but beyond him. He meets certain conditions so that power can be released through him. He is more the channel of power than the creator of it. Therefore, our task as preachers is not so much that of making the sermon powerful as letting it be empowered.

What will allow the sermon to be empowered?

Infused with Prayer

I am glad for the growing social awareness of the church. I take hope in the preaching of the social dimension of our faith, which is often done in our time with courage and relevance. Social involvement is not something alien to the gospel. It is an expression of the gospel. God is concerned with every aspect of human existence and the whole life is to be redeemed. The gospel is addressed not only to the individual man but to the corporate life of men. No human need should be beyond the concern of the church.

Yet, the pulpit with its social concern is not without its danger. The pulpit can be like an army that makes a logistical error, overly extending itself beyond its base of supply. The army may be defeated, not so much from the strength of the enemy, as from low morale and exhaustion.

Basic to the life of the church and pulpit is the conviction that the sources of strength are not merely human. We draw upon the grace and strength of God's life. And prayer is one of the chief vehicles of this power.

The preacher's great mandate to pray is the fact that Jesus Christ prayed. Jesus prayed! He prayed regularly and habitually. He prayed during the routine of living and He met the great crises of His life in prayer.

Prayer may be a high vantage point that allows a sweeping perspective for seeing life whole and complete. Maybe then, more than at any other time, we are able to see life and our world as God sees them. When God had completed His creation, He looked out upon it and declared that it was good. Prayer helps us to make the same declaration. We can affirm that life, despite its evil and pain, has beauty, meaning, and purpose.

As a young man I climbed Mount Mitchell in western North Carolina, which is the highest peak east of the Rockies. The climb was laborious and tiring since I was not accustomed to mountains. I saw little beauty as I climbed the slopes. Here was a deep ravine like a cruel wound in the side of the mountain. There was a barren, protruding boulder that seemed out of place, and the scrubby trees and underbrush were not inspiring. But once I reached the top, I beheld a scene that was almost breath-taking. The deep ravine, barren boulders, and scrubby underbrush had helped form a pattern of beauty. So with prayer. It gives us a vantage point.

But more important, prayer establishes a vital relationship with God. We can commune with Him, become aware of His presence, know His forgiveness, experience the renewal of His grace, and offer our lives to Him in a fuller service. And in becoming aware of Him, there is a heightened awareness of our world and a greater sensitivity to our fellows.

Phillips Brooks used to say that a preacher should go often from the presence of Christ into the presence of men. Prayer is one of the surest ways of doing that. And when we do, we go with a greater power. For lack of a better word, let us call it a radiance.

When Moses came down from Mount Sinai, where he had been in the presence of God, Aaron and others observed that his face shone. Yet, "Moses did not know that the skin of his face shone because he had been talking with God" (Exod. 34:29, RSV). It was not a power that turned Moses' life in upon itself, but released him to more effective leadership and service.

The radiance of which I speak is not the sickly light of a shallow piety. It is not an ascetic look or a holy voice. It is power born of encounter with the living God, who enables the preacher to affirm the basic goodness and purpose of life as well as the healing and reconciling forces that are at work in the brokenness and separation of life. It is confidence, hope, and serenity that have their own quality of light.

If a preacher wants his preaching to be powerful, let him infuse it with prayer.

Enlivened by Personality

We remember Phillips Brooks' famous definition of preaching: "Preaching is the bringing of truth through personality."[1] Brooks wrote again: "The sermon is truth and man together; it is truth brought through man. The personal element is essential."[2] John Knox has emphasized the same truth about preaching. "The preacher is not an expert in religion informing interested learners," he wrote, "but a person sharing some of his most intimate and profound experience with other persons. Preaching is not speech about religion; it is a religious person speaking."[3]

Helmut Thielicke, more recently, has stressed the same truth: "The conventional vocabulary of church language is deceiving or —to express it in psychological terms—that the words of 'sin' and 'grace' no longer 'attract' unless they have first passed through the medium of a living human being transformed, so that he himself is a confession and a witness."[4]

I am thinking of a small chapel I like to visit. It has beautiful windows of abstract art. No figures or obvious patterns appear in them. I have never seen more gorgeous colors than those which appear in them about four o'clock in the afternoon. But these windows are not the source of the light that makes them beautiful. The source is beyond them. As the light passes through them it takes upon itself something of their quality and character. The light is made warmer, richer, and more colorful.

---

1. Op. cit., p. 15
2. Ibid., p. 158
3. John Knox, *The Integrity of Preaching* (New York and Nashville: Abingdon Press, 1957), p. 59
4. Op. cit., p. 47

Those chapel windows are suggestive of preaching. The preacher is not the source of the truth of the gospel. The source is beyond him. Yet, he is the channel and medium of the gospel. As the gospel passes through his mind, heart, will, and imagination, it is enlivened. It should have vividness, vitality, and life that it could not have without the personality of the preacher.

The preacher should give the gospel the finest intellectual expression he can. He should read good books, meet great minds, undergo disciplined study, and ground himself in Biblical truth. I have known too many preachers who felt that the gospel is anti-intellectual, that there is irreconcilable conflict between faith and reason. Paul said that "it pleased God by the foolishness of preaching to save them that believe" (I Cor. 1:21), but he did not say that we are to preach foolishness. There is a vast difference between the two.

It is true that the gospel has been disclosed, not rationally discovered. This does not mean, however, that the gospel is anti-rational, but that its source lies beyond rational powers. When it is preached, the preacher is under the necessity of expressing it in some kind of rational categories. Men are rational beings, and communication demands rational forms. Every preacher, therefore, should want the gospel, as it passes through his mind, to be given the very best rational expression possible.

The gospel must pass through the preacher's heart if the sermon is to have emotional power. Unless the sermon has this quality, it will be cold and without human warmth. The sermon should glow. This is possible since what a preacher confronts in the gospel is not cold intellectual ideas, but a warm, accepting person. He has met a great love that is almost overwhelming and a grace that accepts him just as he is. His heart should have been strangely warmed. Every preacher should realize that the heart, not the head, is the most dynamic side of human personality. Unless he can preach with heart power, the people who hear him will not be moved.

The will of the preacher must also be a factor in the medium of the gospel. The nature of Christian faith involves the will. Faith is not basically climbing the steep ascent of ideas, nor the surge of strong feeling. As already suggested, faith is meeting and encounter. And it is through his volitional powers that the preacher translates the gospel into ethical and social action. He must be, not only a preacher, but a doer of the gospel. People need to see the gospel in the preacher as well as hear it from his lips.

The preacher should also allow the gospel to pass through his imagination, and he has no better example than his Lord. Jesus enlivened truth with his imagination. He put truth in concrete forms, set it in motion, gave it color, and made it vivid and alive. For example, Jesus did not talk abstractly about man's lostness. Man is like a lost sheep, a lost coin, or a lost son. God is more than a principle of love. He is like a seeking shepherd, a searching woman, or a waiting father.

The use of imagination in the pulpit is not without its danger. When divorced from reality and allowed to run wild, it is indeed dangerous. Few things desecrate the truth more than unrestrained imagination. It must be disciplined by integrity and held to reality. To the servant of truth it is a great asset, with a strange power to make the gospel come alive.

Strengthened by Depth

Some preachers major on the unusual, novel, dramatic, even bizarre. This may appeal for a while, but the appeal will pass. It lacks integrity and depth.

Some preachers are aware of the now—the present mood that will soon pass. They ask questions the next generation may not ask; they recognize that situations today may undergo radical change. They speak to people in transition who need help and guidance. This preachers ought to do.

The preacher, however, must be concerned with more than the novel and passing. He must preach to the deep and abiding needs of men.

"Is there not a level in man in which is the same in all," asks Helmut Thielicke, "that level where he is desperate and lonely, despairing of the meaning of existence, but also where he loves children, cherishes his fondest wishes, and hopes for the fulfillment of his dreams? Is there not a dimension where all men are identical and homogeneous?"[5]

Yes, there is that deep level where all men are the same. Man is threatened with meaninglessness and insignificance. He is lonely and he is estranged from God and his brother. He is proud and

---

5. Ibid., p. 23

boastful, yet he is fearful and anxious. He is guilty and he dies. But he feels the need to love, believe, and hope. He dreams of a better race of men and a better world, and puts forth some effort toward achieving those ends. These deep needs may be accented differently in terms of culture, time, and place, but all men everywhere experience them.

We agree, therefore, that preaching must be concerned "with the deep and universal questions: life and death, courage and fear, love and hate, trust and doubt, guilt and forgiveness, pain and joy, shame, remorse, compassion, and hope."[6]

Vitalized by the Holy Spirit

I remember when I realized that next to Jesus Christ, the Holy Spirit is the greatest reality in the New Testament. That realization made a great difference in my theology and preaching.

However, the Holy Spirit is not confined to the New Testament. William Barclay can speak of the men of the Bible as "Men of the Spirit."[7] Wheeler Robinson, who did such a definitive work on the Holy Spirit, could say: "The Bible is the Book of the Spirit. On its first page there is painted the impressive picture of chaos, when darkness was upon the face of the deep; but the Spirit of God was brooding like a mother-bird, upon the face of the waters. From the last page there rings out the evangelical challenge of the church in the world, 'The Spirit and the bride say, Come.' "[8]

The Spirit of God does many things, but chiefly He gives vitality and power.

Ezekiel, through a vision, looked out upon a desert where once a battle raged (chap. 37). The dead had not been removed from the battle field, and their only remains were their bleached bones. There is nothing as dead as bleached bones upon desert sands. God asked Ezekiel: "Son of man, can these bones live?", and Ezekiel answered, "O Lord God, thou knowest." (v. 3, RSV). God breathed his spirit across those dry bones, and living men stood to their feet. Those bleached bones were Ezekiel's nation.

---

6. Henry Grady Davis, *Design for Preaching* (Philadelphia: Fortress Press, 1958), p. 43

7. William Barclay, *The Promise of the Spirit* (Philadelphia: The Westminster Press, 1960), Chapter I, pp. 11-20

8. H. Wheeler Robinson, *The Christian Experience of the Holy Spirit* (London: Nisbet & Co., Ltd., Third edition, 1952), p. 5

It seemed so dead, but God could make it live again. The Spirit of God gives vitality, power, and life.

The apostles became aware of the Holy Spirit as power. After the Resurrection, the disciples were poised for their world mission. But they must wait. ". . . but stay in the city," Jesus told them, "until you are clothed with power from on high" (Luke 24:49, RSV). When the Holy Spirit was given on Pentecost, He came from heaven "like the rush of a mighty wind." He came with power.

There can be no doubt that the New Testament sees preaching as that which is vitalized and empowered by the Holy Spirit. Simon Peter, without the gifts of rhetoric, preached with extraordinary power. As he preached, men cried out: "Brethren, what shall we do?" (Acts 2:37, RSV). Paul, in writing to the Corinthian church, could say, "My speech and my message were not in plausible words of wisdom, but in demonstration of the Spirit and power" (I Cor. 2:4, RSV).

The modern preacher has to make up his mind about the Holy Spirit. Is he reality or a delusion? Does man, from his loneliness, project his desire for a presence and, out of his weakness, imagine that power has been given him? Or is the Holy Spirit the living God, present in our world, mighty to enable our lives and empower our preaching? I believe He is reality.

How will the ancient event of God's saving action become redemptive through today's sermon? That is the great question of preaching. The answer lies in the Holy Spirit more than anywhere else. "The Spirit makes the ancient event in a very real sense an event now transpiring, and the preaching, is a medium of the Spirit's action in doing so. In the preaching, when it is truly itself, the event is continuing or recurring. God's revealing action in Christ is, still or again, actually taking place."[9]

We are often like stranded barges; we have to wait for the tide of God's spirit. Frequently we are like sail boats, with no breeze blowing, but we can lift and unfurl our sails in the expectancy that the winds of God will blow again.

We cannot command the Holy Spirit. He is God's gift, and God chooses when He will give Him to us. But we can wait for Him, long for Him, pray for Him, and expect Him. He will come!

There are many prophets of doom concerning preaching. The

---

9. John Knox, op. cit., p. 12

pulpit, as we have known it, will pass, and preaching will be changed beyond recognition, they tell us. But one thing we should remember: God has chosen to take "what we preach to save those who believe." That is as true now as it ever was. But let us be sure that we put ourselves in the line of power.

8 / PREACHING WITHIN THE CHURCH

IN TIME OF CRISIS IN THE PULPIT, THE PREACHER CAN EASILY become confused, overly anxious, and depressed about preaching. He may be tempted to leave the pulpit and do something else which, he believes, will put him more vitally in touch with people and his world. But he should realize that preaching, even during a pulpit crisis, is the most viable thing the church does.

"Preaching, far from being obsolete, is the most persistent of all church activities," declares George E. Sweazey. "When a church dies, the last thing to be given up is the assembly for worship and preaching. When it is said, 'People are not coming to hear sermons like they used to,' it must be sadly added, 'And even fewer are coming for the rest of what the church would like to do. . . .' The great times for the church have always been times of great preaching, and the reverse is also true. There has never been a widespread upsurge of vigor in the church that was not accompanied by new life in the pulpits. Although every new way of communication should be explored eagerly, the 25 minutes of uninterrupted access to the ears of a roomful of people is still a minister's great opportunity."[1]

Let the modern preacher take hope, but not in a light and fool-hearted way. He will have to ask himself some very agonizing questions, undergo a stern discipline, and be open to the power of God's spirit. His pulpit can be a place of integrity and power where he fulfills his responsibility to his people and his Lord.

---

1. George E. Sweazey, *The Christian Ministry,* January, 1972, p. 6

How can the modern preacher fulfill his responsibility in the pulpit? How can he best use his pulpit to keep his church authentic and nurture his people to Christian maturity?

What Is the Church

The preacher must ask many times from his pulpit, What is the church? He must give a Biblical answer, while being aware of where the church is now. The church must establish its own identity. It must know who it is and what it is to do. Unless there is a strong self-awareness of its uniqueness, it can easily yield to two powerful temptations: to turn in upon itself, and to become like the culture about it.

Richard Niebuhr has pointed up the danger of introversion. "It loses its character as the church," he wrote, "when it concentrates on itself, worships itself, and seeks to make the love of church the first commandment."[2]

One is afraid that the church has been very vulnerable to this temptation. Many see it as largely serving its own institutional ends rather than the world, and being more concerned about preserving its own life than being a servant church.

Kenneth Chafin also speaks of the church's introversion: "There seems to be an ingrown quality about it, so that nearly everything it does is for itself."[3] Hendrik Kraemer, reflecting on the same problem, has said, "The mind of the church is bent, above all, on its own increase and well-being. It is church-centered. It is self-centered. The interest in the world is at best a side-issue."[4]

The church is also tempted to become like the culture, and it can easily yield to this temptation. In becoming like the world, the church loses its identity. Such a church takes into its own life the values of the culture, sometimes the worst ones, such as class pride and racism, and baptizes them in the name of Jesus Christ. Rather than the church transforming the culture, the culture shapes the church after its own image. When you strip away the religious verbiage and dismantle the ceremonial forms, you find the smiling face of the culture.

---

2. H. Richard Niebuhr, *The Purpose of the Church and Its Ministry* (New York, Evanston, and London): Harper and Row, 1956), p. 30

3. Kenneth Chafin, *Help! I'm a Layman* (Waco: Word Books, 1956), p. 6

4. Hendrik Kraemer, *A Theology of the Laity* (Philadelphia: The Westminster Press, 1958), p. 127

The New Testament tells about such a church, the Church of Laodicea. That church is pictured as saying, ". . . I am rich, I have prospered, and I need nothing." Yet, the Lord of the church said it was ". . . wretched, pitiable, poor, blind, and naked" (Rev. 3:17, RSV). That church was like the city. It had the same kind of values, enjoyed the same kind of success, and relied upon the same kind of security. There was no tension between the church and the city. The church was more like a chamber of commerce than a redemptive fellowship, speaking a cutting word of judgment as well as a healing word of mercy.

Theodore O. Wedel's parable of the lifesaving station that became a club is pertinent here since it illustrates the two temptations of the church with which we are concerned.[5] Wedel says that on a dangerous seacoast where shipwrecks often occurred, there was a crude little lifesaving station that was little more than a hut. There was only one boat, and a small crew kept a tireless and selfless watch over the sea. Many shipwrecked people were saved there, and the lifesaving station grew famous. Some of those who had been saved, as well as others, wanted to join. They gave freely of their time and money. The lifesaving station grew, being equipped with new boats and served by new crews highly trained.

Some of the members, becoming unhappy about the crudeness of their building, felt a more comfortable place should be provided. A more commodious building was erected, the emergency cots replaced by beds, and the new station beautifully decorated and furnished. The atmosphere of a club began to pervade the place. Fewer members now being interested in going to sea on a lifesaving mission; they hired professional lifesaving crews to do the work. The lifesaving motif was kept in the club, and a liturgical lifeboat was used in initiations.

The growing comfort of the place was rudely disturbed one night when a large ship foundered off the coast. The hired crew brought in a boatload of cold, wet, and half-drowned people who were dirty and filthy, some of whom had black and yellow skin. That was too much. The property committee took steps immediately to build a shower house outside the club where victims of the sea could be cleaned up before coming inside.

At the next meeting, a more drastic step was taken. Some of

5. *The Ecumenical Review,* October, 1953

the more prominent and influential members felt that the station had outgrown its original purpose and the lifesaving activities should be dropped since they were so unpleasant and a hindrance to the normal life of the club. There were those who opposed this action, feeling that the only way they could justify their existence was to remain a lifesaving station. Losing their vote, they pulled out and went farther down the coast where they founded another life-saving station.

As the years passed, the new lifesaving station underwent the same change as the first one and became a club. Another life-saving station was founded. And so history continues to repeat it-self. If you should visit that seacoast today, you would find a number of exclusive clubs along the shore. Shipwrecks still occur in those rough waters, but most of the people drown.

One of the signs of hope is that the church is trying to free itself from its cultural bondage and turn to the world as a servant church. But without a clear self-identity, it will not be able to do this. The church is a many-faceted reality (this is why so many metaphors are used in the New Testament to describe it), but we likely come nearest to the truth when we think of it as being the people of God. The church is God's people, to do God's work, in God's world.

The church, as the people of God, is people rather than insti-tution-oriented. It is mobile rather than static. The people of God are a servant people, obeying God, and, because they are, they can serve the world without being in bondage to it. And rather than living an ethereal life, the church walks in the dusty ways of history.

Toward Christian Maturity

The preacher of a church is responsible for guiding and nur-turing his people towards Christian maturity. Paul was especially conscious of this task. He spoke of reaching ". . . mature man-hood, to the measure of the stature of the fullness of Christ" (Eph. 4:13, RSV), and ". . . speaking the truth in love, we are to grow up in every way into him who is the head, even Christ" (Eph. 4:15, RSV).

The preacher will need a clear understanding of Christian maturity. What is Christian maturity, and when do people reach it? People reach Christian maturity when they can freely love God and their fellows. H. Richard Niebuhr saw this as the most basic task of the church. He defined the goal of the church as "the increase among men of the love of God and neighbor."[6]

What, then, must the pastor do to help his people achieve this maturity?

First, he must declare over and over again God's redemptive acts.

When the Hebrew son asked the meaning of the laws, ordinances, and symbols of their history, the Hebrew father was instructed to answer his son like this: "We were Pharoah's slaves in Egypt; and the Lord brought us out of Egypt with a mighty hand" (Deut. 6:21, RSV). The Hebrews never tired of recounting this mighty act of deliverance. This theme ran through all their worship and religious instruction.

The Christian preacher has more to declare. He has the deliverance in which the ancient Hebrew exulted and also the deliverance of the Christ event with its life, death, and resurrection. And his preaching is done within the context of the New Covenant which is written, not upon tablets of stone, but on the hearts of men.

In declaring the mighty acts of God, he will be conscious of an evangelistic task, for unless the people have experienced new life in Christ, there will be no life to mature. Without this, they have only a religious cloak thrown around their old life with its pride, false values, and self-centeredness. They need to be stripped of that cloak so that, in their nakedness, they may turn from their false life to the life that Christ can give, and be clothed in a righteousness that is not of their achieving.

But the saving acts of God have a more specific relation to Christian maturity. A child cannot grow and mature unless he knows that he is loved, accepted, and secure. Just so with the Christian. Christians cannot grow if they are enslaved by guilt and fear and unless they know themselves to be loved and accepted by God as well as the fellowship of the church. The redemptive action of God sets them free from sin and guilt. Its more positive function is the assurance that they are loved, accepted, and made secure in Christ.

Paul, in the closing part of the eighth chapter of Romans, runs

---

6. Op. cit., p. 31

the full gamut of hazards and tragedy, and then draws this wonderful conclusion: Nothing in all creation "will be able to separate us from the love of God in Christ Jesus our Lord." (Rom. 8:39, RSV). In this love of God, from which no power can ever separate him, the Christian can grow into maturity.

Second, the preacher must seek a response of the total life to the gospel.

While he will address the gospel to the wholeness of persons, the response will involve the intellect, emotion, will, and spiritual capacity.

Any one of these areas left undeveloped will leave the person immature and unbalanced in his Christian life. Without intellectual growth, religious faith may degenerate into magic or superstition. We are to love God with our minds. Unless there is a response of the heart, the religious life will be cold and lifeless, lacking warmth and power. Unless there is a response of the will, the religious life can be coldly intellectual or effervescent with feeling, but lacking in ethical concern, which is one of the basic dimensions of great religion. We are to love our neighbors as ourselves. There must be a response of the spiritual capacity in the awareness of God's presence in the world in the person of the Holy Spirit. The Holy Spirit is an enabling presence without which the Christian cannot be truly strong and effective. It is only as there is a total response of the whole person in love and obedience to Jesus Christ that the person can grow into Christian maturity.

Third, the preacher must stress the corporate nature of the church.

No one grows into Christianity alone anymore than one grows in personal maturity in social isolation. The church is more than individuals, brought into casual relationships through worship, study, fellowship, and ministry. Paul's metaphor of the church as being the body of Christ is helpful here. Members of the church are people centered in Jesus Christ, whose lives are inextricably interrelated. There is a caring, supporting, healing, and nurturing relationship within the church. Like the human body, members of the church are organically related. When one member is sick, the whole church is affected, and strength and vitality are rushed from the whole body so the sick one can be well again. No one is free to do as he pleases, yet everyone is free in the love and acceptance of the others. All are dependent on the whole body, yet each is indispensable, even the most humble and insignificant person. No one is independent. If an arm is to survive and be healthy, it must remain a part of the body. If severed from the body, the arm will die. Just so with the individual Christian. He must be nurtured and sustained by the body of Christ which is the church.

Fourth, the preacher must create tension in the life of the church.

Tension is one of the signs of life, and it is one of the marks of growing and maturing things. The church that is growing in maturity cannot escape tension. The gospel is tension producing. There will be tension between where the church is and where it should be, what the church is and what it should become. There will be tension between the church as an institution and a redemptive fellowship. There will be tension between the priestly and prophetic roles. There will be tension between the personal dimension and social demands of the gospel. There will be tension between the church and the culture as the church seeks to keep its identity, yet be relevant to the world. And there will be tension between the freedom the church seeks for itself and the Lordship of Jesus Christ that is over it.

It becomes the responsibility of every preacher, therefore, to keep a maximum tension in the life of his church. Yet, a word of caution is needed here. All tensions are not creative. Many are destructive by their very nature. Even creative tension, when heightened beyond a certain degree, can be destructive. The pastor must have mature wisdom, a deep love and concern for his people, and sensitivity to the Holy Spirit in order to determine how much tension his church can stand. This difficult task is laid upon him, and he shirks it at great detriment to his church and himself.

Both Priest and Prophet

The preacher, if he is to fulfill his ministry in the pulpit, must be both priest and prophet.

As priest, the preacher represents his people before God, prays for them, leads their worship, comforts them, loves and cares for them, counsels them, and performs many ministries that are supporting and healing. He will be a priest in the pulpit. This means that much of his preaching will be pastoral in nature. There will be a nurturing, supporting, and healing quality in his sermons and he must see preaching as a basic act of worship. "Preaching is primarily an act of worship. Preaching is glorifying God who, in Christ, came for us men and for our salvation."[7]

But the preacher must also be the prophet in the pulpit. He must often speak God's word of judgment over the pride, prejudice, and false values of his people and their society as well as his own life. As prophet in the pulpit, he does not spare himself.

There is tension between the priest and prophet. When the priest and prophet meet they usually don't like each other. They threaten each other.

You remember the confrontation between Amaziah the priest of Bethel and Amos the prophet. Amaziah was concerned with the sanctuary at Bethel and the people who worshiped there. He did not feel his business was to dismantle the altar. He wanted the sanctuary to be strong. His primary duty, as he saw it, was not the reforming of society but helping the people to develop a certain style of spiritual life as well as keeping a religious institution powerful. Amos spoke God's judgment over the people and blasted the social evils. When the two men met there was instant conflict. Amaziah said to Amos, "O seer, go, flee away to the land of Judah, and eat bread there, and prophesy there, but never again prophesy at Bethel, for it is the king's sanctuary, and it is a temple of the kingdom" (Amos 7:12-13, rsv).

The preacher feels the tension between the priest and prophet in his own life. The tension is always uncomfortable, sometimes almost unbearable. So, we usually relax the tension by accenting the priest within us, and we make a caricature of our role by allowing the priest to be overdrawn. One of our great needs is to have the image of the preacher redrawn in such a way that the priest and prophet will be held in proportion and balance.

I have already spoken of the need of creative tension within the life of the church. If a pastor should ask how he can best create that tension, I believe the best answer is to be both priest and prophet. When he has the courage to be both, the tension in his own life will stimulate tension in all the life of his church.

With an Eye to the World

The preacher must not yield to the temptation of allowing his church to be an in-group, carefully insulated from the world. His

---

7. Ford, op. cit., p. 71

people must not shuttle back and between from the sanctuary and their secular life as if they were two worlds, separate and far removed from each other. As he preaches to his people, even about things intimate to the life of the fellowship, he must be aware of the larger world into which his people will soon be thrust. He must help them realize that as they leave the place of worship they will be no less the church when scattered into the many areas of the community's life. They go there as witnesses to the things in which they most deeply believe and as people on a mission of reconciliation.

D. W. Cleverly Ford has written of the relationship of preaching in the pulpit and mission in the world. "This represents a high doctrine of the church preaching," he says, "but not so that the church is treated as an in-group. On the contrary, preaching is counted as integral to mission. The preaching takes place in church so that the world which is not in the church may hear. . . . Preaching viewed as witness prevents preaching from ceasing at the church doors. It links it to mission. Preaching is and always has been the inspiration of mission. When preaching is at a low ebb, mission is at a low ebb. Conversely, when mission is at a low ebb, preaching is at a low ebb. Preaching leads to mission. It leads to it because witness forms part of it."[8]

I have spoken of the danger of a church succumbing to the influence of its culture. There is nothing more tragic than a church that is secular at the center of its life, yet carefully insulated from the real life of the world. This often happens. The preacher must help his church purge itself of its own secularism and at the same time become truly worldly. "In other words, it has to become in a new way unworldly and worldly in one."[9]

Let the preacher take seriously his task in the pulpit as he preaches within the church. Let him know that if his church dies, the pulpit will be the last thing to pass. Let him know, also, that, if his church is to be renewed, the pulpit will likely be the first place to experience new life. As he takes seriously his task, let him perform it in hope.

---

8. Ibid., pp. 71, 75
9. Kraemer, op. cit., p. 166

9 / PREACHING BEYOND THE CHURCH

THE CHURCH HAS BEEN TETHERED TOO CLOSELY TO SACRED BUILD-
ings, holy hours, and religious seasons. It needs to be released
to a greater freedom and mobility beyond ecclesiastical walls so that
it may be a redemptive mission in the world.

We have asked, "How do you get them in?" That is an important question. If nothing vital happens within the hours of
worship, training, and fellowship, nothing of significance is likely
to happen anywhere else. But we must also ask, "How do you send
them out?" We must realize that God intends the world, not
sacred buildings, to be the real habitat of the church.

One of the great responsibilities of the preacher is to help the
gospel be heard and lived beyond the institutional church. That
may be his greatest task. How will he do it? This is one of the most
serious questions with which he will have to wrestle.

The Servant Church

The preacher must help the church to see itself as a servant.

Possibly the most startling thing about the Christian faith is
this: When the great God of our universe was ready to let men
know who He really is and what He is like, He came in the form
of a servant. "God was in Christ" (II Cor. 5:19), and Jesus Christ
"emptied himself, taking the form of a servant" (Phil. 2:7).

The church must learn that, if it is to be like its Lord, it must
be a servant. Jesus Christ was. Servanthood was unmistakably His
basic role. He said of Himself: "even as the Son of man came not

to be served but to serve, and give his life as a ransom for many" (Matt. 20:28, RSV). But for fear his disciples would not understand, He dramatized His role as a servant. At the last meal Jesus had with His disciples before His crucifixion, He asked for a towel and basin of water. He then washed and dried their dirty feet. He was their servant.

Jesus was careful to point out to His followers that greatness lay in service and that they must be servants. "Whoever would be great among you must be your servant," He told them, "and whoever would be first among you must be your slave" (Matt. 20:26-27, RSV).

The early church took seriously the admonition of its Lord to be a servant. Paul spoke of himself as being a slave of Jesus Christ, but this was no more true of him than the whole church. The church could not do otherwise and be true to Jesus Christ, knowing that its Lord was a servant.

J. C. Hoekendijk has spoken of the servant role of the church. "There are, in my judgment," he writes, "the three directional words: self-emptying, service, solidarity with the people. And, of course, each of these words, as well as the three of them together, points to the Servant of the Lord, as portrayed in Isaiah: the prototype of all that he called 'Messianic', the model of the Messianic congregations."[1]

Yet, the church is tempted to seek power. It is easily enamored with status symbols and prestige. It often seeks to be lord rather than servant. It should resist stoutly this temptation, but, when it yields, it should be quick to confess its sin and ask for God's forgiveness. The way of the church is not that of the prince, general, political boss, or business tycoon. Its way is that of the servant. It has been served by its Lord. Therefore, it must serve. It must always ask for a towel and basin of water.

Sent into the World

The preacher must help direct the servant church into the world.

Jesus sustained a double-action relationship with His disciples. He constantly called them to Himself for worship, instruction and fellowship, but He always sent them away, back into the world.

---

1. J. C. Hoekendijk, *The Church Inside Out* (Philadelphia: The Westminster Press, 1946), p. 71

I am thinking of a congregation that worships in a sanctuary where the focal points of worship are the cross and a resurrection window. These symbols keep before them the redemption wrought through Christ's death and the victory won through His resurrection. At the close of the worship, when they turn to leave the sanctuary, they face a facade window which is the artist's interpretation of the Great Commission. They see an elliptical world superimposed with an open Bible and the cross. At the bottom of the window is a fish in a stylized wave, symbolizing baptism, and at the top is a descending dove, representing the Holy Spirit that empowers for mission. When the congregation takes that window seriously, they know that their task is not ending at the door. It is just beginning there. During the past hour, their vision should have been clarified and their lives invigorated for their mission in the world.

One of the signs of hope is the growing awareness that the church must live its life basically in the world. Yet, the leaving of its cloistered life for the rough-and-tumble world is painful. Often there is real hesitancy to venture forth.

A few summers ago I heard chimed over the life of a modern town a nostalgic tune from the tower of one of the leading churches. The tune, "The Little Brown Church in the Vale," awoke in my mind an image of a quiet and sequestered church withdrawn from the strife and tension of life. There was something in me that made me want to go back to that church which is really too idyllic ever to have existed. I often need a place of refuge, and that church was a symbol pointing to such a haven. Yet, I knew I could never go back. The winds of change and crisis are blowing the church from its safe and sheltered life, and these winds are omens of hope. I know that "all over the world, the necessity of leaving our safe church harbors and of putting to sea again is indelibly printed in our minds."[2]

The Assembly of the World Council of Churches, almost twenty years ago, said: "The real battles of faith today are being fought in factories, shops, offices, and farms, in political parties, and government agencies, in countless homes, in the press, in radio, television, in the relationships of nations. Very often it is said the church should go into these spheres, but the fact is that the church

---

2. Ibid, p. 15

is already in these spheres in the persons of the laity."[3] This is as true today as it was then.

God intended from the beginning that the real battles of faith should be fought in the world. It was the world God loved and to it he gave His only begotten Son. It was the world God was reconciling to Himself through Jesus Christ (II Cor. 5:19). God's mighty thrust in Jesus Christ was out there in the world.

Jesus fulfilled his ministry basically in the world. He was driven from the synagogue, and was crucified almost within the shadow of the temple where He found some of His strongest opposition. Religious people were offended at Him, but, while Jesus was disappointed in their rejection of Him, He was not frustrated because his mission was fulfilled basically outside organized religion. The world seemed to be a natural habitat for His gospel and ministry. He called His disciples from fishing boats and tax offices. What worldly places! His classroom was a fishing boat or ledge of rock; His pulpit, a wayside. His language was more secular than theological. He died at a crossroads of the ancient world so cosmopolitan that they wrote His accusation, nailed to His cross, in three languages—Hebrew, Greek, and Latin.

Jesus knew how tempted religious people are to withdraw from the crudeness, brokenness, and pain of the world. In His parable of the Good Samaritan, Jesus answered the question, Who is my neighbor? But He did more than that. His parable was also a judgment against the organized religion of His time. It was too insensitive to the pain of the world and too concerned about its own welfare and comfort. The first person who passed the robbed and wounded man by the wayside was a priest. The next man who passed by the unfortunate victim was a Levite, who was a kind of church administrator. Both of them were religious functionaries of the Temple at Jerusalem. The priest and Levite may have performed perfectly at the Temple the following Sabbath, but the world has never bothered to remember what they did. Yet, the world will never forget what they refused to do—minister to a robbed and wounded man.

Wherever we find human pain we find a holy place. It may be more holy than an altar of prayer. It is a holy place, not because pain is holy. The pain may have been caused by the most obvious

3. Evanston Assembly Report (World Council of Churches, 1954), See VI, p. 11

sin. It is holy because God is there, binding up and healing. His church should also be there.

We should remember that the interior life of the church is tested by its life in the world. The test of the altar is the work bench. The test of the eleven o'clock hour of worship on Sunday morning is the long hours of the week. The test of the life of the sanctuary is the life we live in the world. The test of our meeting God is the way we meet men. The test of being forgiven, often mediated through worship, is our willingness to forgive. The test of our salvation by grace is how graciously we deal with our fellows. The most spiritually rarefied experiences are to be tested along the dusty ways of human involvement.

As the church seeks to fulfill its mission in the world, it should recall a metaphor from the New Testament—the church as a pilgrim people. The pilgrim cannot settle down. He is destined to be on the move. He can never buy a plot of land and say, "I will build a house and spend my life here." Since he is a traveler, he will spend his life in inns, hostels, and motels. His life, rather than being stationary, will have mobility. So the church in the world must have mobility. It must be sensitive to SOS calls, many of which are almost muffled, and be able to move quickly to places of loneliness, pain, and tragedy.

Through the Laity

The preacher must be very conscious of the laity and give time to equipping them for ministry in the world. The servant church, if it goes into the world, will go through its laity. The voice of the preacher can carry far through them.

I remember worshiping one Sunday morning in the First Congregational Church of Williamstown, Massachusetts. What impressed me most about the service was the church bulletin. It was captioned: "The Meeting House of the First Congregational Church." The building was not the church, but the meeting house where the church met for worship, study, and fellowship. Below the caption was a picture of the beautiful colonial structure. At the bottom were the names of the pastor and associate pastor. Then the ministers. And who were they? "All members of First Congregational Church." The laity were the ministers. They were there for an hour of worship, and soon they would be scattered throughout the life of that New England town. Ideally, they would go into every segment of that community's life as the servants of Christ. They would be the church in the world.

The church of our time is not only finding its mission in the world again. It is also discovering its laity. Kenneth Chafin has said that "the discovery of the laity as the church's greatest resource for ministry is the greatest discovery of this day."[4]

Yet, the growing significance of the laity in the modern church is more rediscovery than discovery. From the beginning there has been a strong theological basis for the ministry of laymen. (The terms *laymen* and *laity* will be used interchangeably).

As you read the New Testament, you meet laymen, with the possible exception of Paul. The disciples of Jesus were laymen. They had never attended a theological seminary, and no hands of ordination had been laid on their heads.

You do not find a marked distinction between clergy and laity in the New Testament. But something tragic, which began at the close of the first Christian century, has continued to this day. Two distinct classes arose within the church—the clergy and the laity. These two classes reflected the duality of the Graeco-Roman society which was composed of the magistrate (*kleros*) and the people *(laos)*. Our term *clergy* is derived from *kleros* while our term *laity* comes from *laikos,* which is derived from *laos. Laikos* literally means belonging to the people, common. In a city state, the magistrates were the governing class while the people were the governed. The magistrates were the administrators of justice, the people the recipients of justice. Authority was vested in the magistrates, not the people.

The secular duality was taken into the structure of the church and given a religious sanction. The clergy administered grace through the sacraments while the laity was the recipient of grace. The clergy was subject while the laity was object. The clergy was active, the laity passive. The clergy was superior, the laity inferior. The clergy was a tiny minority, yet a preponderance of power and authority was placed in their hands. The clergy was the church while the laity was a kind of accessory to the church.

Throughout the history of the church there have been attempts to overcome this dualism. The Protestant Reformation was a notable example with its doctrine of the priesthood of believers.

---

4. Op. cit., p. 97

The doctrine pointed in the right direction, yet the effort was abortive. The dualism remains to this day.

Once more with a serious return to Biblical theology, history presents us with the opportunity of overcoming this dualism. The modern preacher has no greater opportunity than that of helping heal the breach. The church is essentially the people of God. God through Christ calls men from all nations, classes, and races to be his people. We become the people of God, not by our own goodness or initiative. God calls us in grace to be His people. This is the prior and basic call, and until that call is recognized, no other call really matters. The call is comprehensive, embracing both laity and clergy. All are called to be the servants of God. Therefore, the layman is just as much a minister as the clergyman.

The clergy and laity alike are called to the basic mission of the church, that of reconciliation. Paul, writing to the laity of Corinth, could say that God "gave us the ministry of reconciliation . . . entrusting to us the message of reconciliation. So we are ambassadors for Christ" (II Cor. 5:18-20, RSV).

Traditionally, we have thought of the laymen aiding the minister, but maybe just the opposite should be true. The greatest task of the minister may well be that of equipping the laymen for ministry in the world which is likely the basic meaning of Ephesians 4:12, (RSV). When the first comma in the traditional punctuation is removed, it reads like this: "For the equipment of the saints for the work of the ministry, for building up the body of Christ."

The minister, in helping to equip the laymen for ministry, must guard against the real danger of clericalizing the laymen. Laymen must not become replicas of the clergy. Sometimes this happens. Laymen may develop a pious tone, a sanctimonious manner, or a holy air. They may become pale shadows of a certain type of clergy they have known. When this happens, it is most unfortunate. Such laymen lose rapport with the world where they are called to minister. They become misfits in their own world. Therefore, the ministers must help the laymen keep their own individuality, robustness, and down-to-earth quality. Hoekendijk puts it this way: "I want to put it sharply: a clericalized layman is unsuited for the apostolate; he has become a church-domesticated layman, tamed and caged by the church—one who has betrayed his own trade and has become unfaithful to the earth."[5]

5. Op. cit., p. 89

To Evangelize in the Secular

The servant church must go into the world, through its laity, to do evangelism in the secular life.

This is to evangelize where laymen live. They live in the world. They stand at the crowded crossroads of life and they are where the action is. They beat and fashion burning issues on secular anvils. They live where the claims of mammon are more clamoring than the claims of God. It is crucial for them to know what it is to be the people of God there.

Such evangelism will not be separate from the job. It will be an integral part of the layman's work, not an evangelism that is done essentially during leisure or spare time. It will be an evangelism practiced on and through the job. It will be expressed through how the laymen feel about their jobs, their values as reflected in their work, their priorities, and the relationships they establish with those with whom they work.

Relationships will be crucial for evangelism in the secular world. Laymen will know that God has called them to be more than honest, industrious, thrifty, and frugal. They will never be less than these, but there is nothing distinctively Christian about these homely virtues. They must know a love that enables them to identify with the loneliness, pain, and brokenness of the world. They will accept people for what they are and believe in them for what they can become. They will give strength to the weak, hope to the discouraged, and comfort to the sorrowing. They will never use and manipulate people. They will always respect the freedom and dignity of persons. They will not widen the cleavages between men, but will span them with good will, understanding, and acceptance. They will not gouge the wounds of the world but will try to heal them. They will, without pride or self-righteousness, be conscious of belonging to the new order which has been thrust into the midst of the old. They will confess through their deep, caring, and healing relationships that Jesus Christ is Lord.

In this evangelism, the deed will precede the word. Laymen will try to be the love and acceptance of Christ before they make a verbal witness. But the word, growing out of these relationships, can be very effective. There will be a place for verbal witnessing. People, touched by the influence of Christian laymen, will, sooner or later, ask the meaning of their style of life. Then they will have the opportunity to bear their witness in a very direct and personal manner. Out of their loving relationships they can tell of God's love; out of their gracious relationships they can tell of God's grace in Christ; out of their accepting relationships, they can tell of how Christ accepts us just as we are.

Few things should give the preacher greater heart than to know that his voice need not be silenced at 12:00 o'clock noon on Sunday. While his pulpit is set within the life of the church, the message he preaches can be carried into every segment of the community's life through laymen. Let, therefore, every preacher give serious attention to his laymen. They share with him the task of preaching beyond the church.

10 / PREACHING TO INDIVIDUAL MAN

PREACHING MUST BE DIRECTED TO INDIVIDUAL MAN. IN A SENSE, HE is the ultimate goal of preaching. The gospel has the power to touch deep, inner springs of feeling and action, and, unless it does, the thrust of the sermon will have been dissipated before it reaches its main goal.

Preaching should not be addressed to the individual apart from the social context of his life. Man is not only individual. He is corporate as well. The individual is involved with many people in many relationships. Out of these relationships he has become who he is. His life is a shared venture. Yet, the sources of social life are individuals. They are the springs of corporate life. Therefore, preaching must be concerned with these primary sources and springs of life.

Individual Man

Two basic poles of human existence are individual and corporate man. Both are real. Neither must be denied, nor the one sacrificed for the other.

Individual man is unique. He can never be duplicated. Even his fingerprints are distinctive. Among the three billion human beings who inhabit this planet there will be no fingerprints just like his.

The individual person undergoes suffering common to men everywhere. He experiences physical pain, mental anguish, and spiritual suffering. Yet, his suffering is not that of mankind. It is his own. It has stamped upon it his own individuality.

Every individual has worth, dignity, and value. He is not to be used as a means to an end. He is not to be used as a tool, nor manipulated as if he were a thing.

The Bible was written against the background of a culture that placed far greater stress on the corporate life than we do. We accent the individual while that culture accented the community. Yet, the individual is constantly emerging and asserting himself throughout the Bible.

The Word of God in the Bible is normally addressed to the corporate life of a people, yet that word is often given initially to the individual in clear and compelling accent. A vision is frequently given to an individual long before the community or nation even dimly sees it. An individual experiences the judgment and mercy of God, and then tells the nation about the God who wounds in judgment and heals in mercy. How often the individual's personal encounter with God becomes the turning point of the nation.

We remember Moses meeting God on the backside of a desert. The possibility of emancipation occurred when Moses encountered God, not in the vision of enslaved people. Isaiah experienced God in the Temple, and the intimate personal moment came when God said to him: "Behold, this has touched your lips; your guilt is taken away, and your sin forgiven" (Isa. 6:7, RSV). Out of this event came a radically new direction of life which made such a strong impact on his nation. Jeremiah, who had the ear of his nation across a generation, began his prophetic ministry with a personal encounter with God. "Behold, I have put my words in your mouth," God told him (Jer. 1:9, RSV). Amos, the rustic from Tekoa who blasted without mercy the social evils of a nation, often went back to the great moment of his life when ". . . the Lord took me from following the flock, and the Lord said to me, 'Go, prophesy to my people Israel' " (Amos 7:15, RSV).

Paul, who did so much to help call forth the new people of God, had a shattering encounter with God. His old life was demolished so that he might become a new man in Christ. That transforming experience began when the living Christ addressed him by name.

We remember how person-centered the ministry of Jesus was. Some of His most dramatic and meaningful experiences came from face to face relationships. His disciples were led to follow Him out of personal encounters. Who can forget His meeting with Nicodemus, the woman of Samaria, and the Rich Young Ruler? Some of the most significant things he said were offered, not to the crowds, but to individuals.

It is little wonder, then, that great preaching has always been aware of the individual.

Harry Emerson Fosdick once defined preaching as "personal counseling on a group basis."[1] While Fosdick addressed the great social issues of his day, he was always aware of the individual with his hopes and fears, faith and doubt, guilt and striving after a better life. Through the years thousands of people left his services feeling that Fosdick had somehow ferreted them out from his great congregation and spoken to them personally. The sanctuary often became a counseling chamber.

Fosdick on another occasion spoke of a good sermon as being "an engineering operation by which a chasm is bridged so that the spiritual goods on one side—the 'unsearchable riches of Christ'—are actually transported into personal lives upon the other."[2]

Phillips Brooks, considered by many to be the greatest preacher America has produced, warned the preacher: "If he takes his eye off the single soul as the prize he is to win, he loses his best power. All successful preaching," he continued, "I more and more believe, talks to individuals. . . . Let your preaching be to individuals, and to the church always as living for and made up of individuals."[3]

John Knox has stressed the same truth: "Preaching is addressed to individuals and must be aimed at meeting their personal needs. The individuals are, of course, members of communities—of church, of nation, of family, and the like. One cannot speak to them without taking into account the context of the group or corporate existence in which they are involved. But one must speak to them. The wider context is of concern only as it affects them. The individual hearer, in his own personal situation, is the necessary focus of the preacher's attention."[4]

The Individual and His Social Setting

It has already been observed that, as the preacher addresses the gospel to the individual, he must be conscious of the individual's social context. It is dangerous to do otherwise. To see the individual

---

1. *The New York Times,* October 6, 1969
2. Ibid.
3. Op. cit., p. 22
4. Op. cit., p. 71

set apart from the social setting of his life is to see him falsely. His life is inescapably set within a social context. His most individual gifts and powers have been developed within social relationships. He became self-aware as he became aware of others. He learned he was an I by standing over against another person who was a you. His most personal experience has social overtones and carries social responsibilities.

Reference has been made to Isaiah's experience in the Temple, His lips were cleansed, his heart made pure, and his sins forgiven. It was intensely personal. Yet, it all took place within the social context of his life. There was awareness of social involvement and corporate guilt. Standing in the presence of a holy God, he cried out: "Woe is me! For I am lost; for I am a man of unclean lips, and I dwell in the midst of a people of unclean lips . . ." (Isa. 6:5, RSV).

The preacher must be aware of the individual against his immediate social background. He does not preach to men set against the nineteenth-century culture, but to individuals whose lives have been powerfully shaped by a dynamic, technological society.

The individual has experienced a kind of freedom and liberation made possible by his society. He is freer to go, to do, and to achieve than anyone before him, even those in his immediate past. Skills are within his easy reach and he enjoys numerous educational advantages. Never before have so many medical services been offered, and he enjoys various tools and gadgets that relieve his life of drudgery and give him many comforts. His technological society offers him many wonderful things, and he would not like to return to "the good old days."

Yet, the individual finds it increasingly difficult to achieve warm, personal relationships in his society. He frequently feels swallowed up by big organizations that grow faster still. The perforations on an IBM card may tell his story where he works. He can stand in an assembly line, turning a bolt or screw, through years, and never have the satisfaction of completing a single finished product. His life can feel as fragmented and incomplete as the work he does. It lacks wholeness; drives toward creativity are easily stifled. Once he spoke of the skills of craftsmen. Now, more often, he speaks of the sophistication of machines. More and more he lives by decisions made for him and beyond him. The sense of personal mastery over his own life has progressively slipped from him. Anonymity is one of the marks of his time, and many of the forces that shape his life are depersonalizing.

It is little wonder, then, that we are in a crisis of personal identity. The preacher must not expect the crisis to pass hurriedly. It will be with us for a long time. Men will continue to ask, Who am I?

Many people see the small group supplanting the pulpit. One reason for this is that they believe the small group is better able to meet the personal identity crisis. In the small group, the individual is involved in face to face relationships. He is known for who he is, and gets to know other persons. He is able to express himself, and he can know that he is making a contribution. He can feel needed, wanted, and accepted. While the outcome of so many things is beyond him, he can help shape the conclusion drawn by the group. Here he can be a person.

The preacher must further see the personal and social dimensions of the gospel as complementing each other. Preachers sometimes feel that these two dimensions are irreconcilable. But this is to misunderstand the fundamental nature of the gospel. It is both personal and social, and this becomes obvious when the individual is addressed in the social context of his life. The personal gospel may open the door for speaking to crucial social issues without the tragic disruptions that often follow prophetic preaching in our churches today. The pastor who, through his life and preaching, has touched the deep springs of personal life in love and acceptance is best able to preach to the social issues of his day.

John Knox has commented pertinently about this: "For every preacher of the social gospel who is rejected by his congregation, another can be found just as much concerned for social justice and just as forthright in expressing his concern in deed and word whose congregation continues to be loyal to him. The difference lies—not always, by any means, but often—in the fact that in one case social evils and objectives are dealt with in the true personal context of preaching whereas in the other it is not so."[5]

A preacher had dealt courageously with the racial problem in his community, and many of his church were up in arms against him. One night his official board met secretly to deal with the problem. At the beginning of the meeting, it seemed a foregone con-

5. Ibid., p. 72

clusion that the preacher would be fired. As the conversation gathered fierceness and momentum, a man stood up and said, "I cannot vote against my pastor. He stayed up all night with my wife during her last illness." That turned the tide in favor of the pastor, and he was able to stay and continue his ministry as a pastor who loved and cared for his people and as a prophet who dared attack the social evils of the community.

While the mutual acceptance between a pastor and his people is best achieved in pastoral relationships, it can also be achieved from the pulpit. When a preacher preaches a gospel that is genuinely concerned with persons and does it in a caring, accepting, and supporting spirit, relationships can be created that will stand the strain and stress of prophetic preaching.

The Gospel and Personal Needs

A part of the genius of the Christian gospel is its power to speak to the deepest personal needs of people. What, then, are some of these needs to which the gospel must be addressed?

There is the need for meaning. Life is often like a jigsaw puzzle where the pieces will not fit together. There seems to be no pattern. No rhyme, reason, or meaning appears.

Victor Frankl, a prisoner of Hitler's concentration camps during World War II, has founded the third Viennese School of Psychotherapy, which he calls logotherapy. (The two preceding were the Freudian and Adlerian Schools.) Logotherapy is healing through meaning.

As a prisoner, Frankl had his life stripped to its bare and naked existence. His father, mother, brother, and his wife died in camps or were sent to the gas ovens. He and his sister were the only members of his family to survive. What would enable a man to keep his sanity and not fall apart during such tragic barenness? Meaning. The meaning might be as slight as a memory or a faint ray of light that shines into the dark night of the future. He discovered that a man can bear almost any how if he knows the why.

Despite the fact that life is constantly threatened by meaninglessness, our gospel assures us that it has purpose. Life has not been cast up by blind and accidental forces. God has created us. Some purpose runs through all of life. There is work to be done, people to be loved, causes to be championed, a God to be worshiped and served, and a destination to be reached. Man has been set on a journey that ends somewhere.

There is also the need for the individual to feel that his life has worth.

Man is dwarfed by his universe. He is very small and very helpless. His universe, like a heartless machine, will crush him beneath its inexorable wheels. And social situations such as poverty and minority status can make people feel cheap and inferior. The individual may have his self-image so injured that he feels worthless and without significance.

The gospel can give worth to persons. It assures men that they have been created in the likeness of God. "Yet thou hast made him a little less than God," exulted the Psalmist, "and dost crown him with glory and honor" (Ps. 8:5, RSV). It is true that sin has marred that image, almost defacing it in some men. But Christ can restore that image. He can redeem a man to worth. William Barclay has commented, "It was the glory of Christianity that made people who were things into real men and women, nay more, into sons and daughters of God. . . . Christianity was, and still is literally the most uplifting thing in the whole universe."[6]

Celsus, a brilliant and gifted man, was one of the most devastating critics of early Christianity. He jeeringly said that those who followed Jesus were the rag, tag, and bobtail of humanity. "Yes," replied Origen, "but he does not leave them the rag, tag, bobtail of humanity, but out of the material you would have thrown away as useless he fashions men, giving them back their self-respect, enabling them to stand upon their feet and look God in the eye. They were cowed, cringing, broken things. But the Son has made them free."

There is the further need for the individual to have faith in something more powerful, better, and more loving than himself. This does not mean that he decries his gifts and powers, but that he needs a reality beyond himself, constantly and in life's extremities.

I know a man who became a prisoner of the Japanese with the fall of Corregidor during War War II. Having known him earlier, I was glad to see him soon after his return home. While the privation of prison life had reduced his strength, I discovered no cynicism

---

6. William Barclay, *Letters to the Corinthians* (Philadelphia: The Westminster Press, 1954), p. 24

or bitterness. He had a wholesome outlook and faced the future with confidence. He told me of how rapidly character often deteriorated under the stress of life as he had known it. Men frequently stole the meager rationing from their buddies. And often men lay down to die because they did not have the will to live.

I asked him one day what was the secret of his mental balance and hopeful outlook. He shocked me with his simple and spontaneous answer. Faith, he said. Then he told me his story. His camp was located at the base of a mountain that had snow-capped peaks the year round. One morning as he stood in the doorway of the barracks, looking at those snowcapped peaks, a verse of Scripture came to his mind, one which he had learned as a boy in our Sunday School. "I will lift up mine eyes unto the hills, from whence cometh my help. My help cometh from the Lord which made heaven and earth" (Ps. 121:1-2). He said this became a daily ritual of the early morning. That became the basic source of strength for those hard days as a prisoner of war. It never occurred to him that his faith was an escape from the tough reality of his life. Rather, he was bringing reality from beyond himself into the midst of his barren existence.

Our gospel places great value upon man. It has its own kind of humanism. But it never suggests for a moment that man is the highest value, or that he is an end within himself and capable of achieving his own destiny. It recognizes that man needs help from beyond himself, and then gladly announces that such help is available. They who wait upon the Lord renew their strength, and near is the mercy and love of God made known in Jesus Christ.

Again, the individual needs reconciliation. He is like a small island in a strait, separated from the two mainlands—God and man. He is lonely and estranged. He needs to be forgiven of the sin that separates him from God and his brother. He needs his broken relationships healed. He needs to be connected with the two mainlands of his existence. This is possible in Christ since His mission was one of reconciliation.

Still again, the individual needs to love and be loved. There is a sense in which this is his greatest need.

I was explaining the architecture and symbolism in the chancel area of our church to some children. They were extremely restless. Then I began to interpret the resurrection window. Jesus is emerging from the tomb, His right leg having cleared it. His right hand is raised in blessing and in His left hand He carries a banner of victory over death. I explained that Jesus, in raising His right hand in blessing, is telling us that He loves and cares for us. I suddenly realized that the children were caught up in rapt attention. But why? I was saying the thing that the human heart craves most to hear. We want to know that somebody loves and cares for us. Our gospel gives us this assurance. God has taken the initiative in love. He has loved us first, and, since He has, we can love. We can become the channel of His love for the healing of our world.

Our gospel has the power to create a fellowship of love where we are accepted and cared for just as we are. It is in this fellowship that the personal identity crisis of our time can best be met.

Finally, the individual wants the assurance of a continuing life. He does not want to believe that the journey of life is into darkness and nothingness. He does not want to be like a candle blown out by a careless and impersonal wind. He has longings in his heart for eternal things. He wants fulfillment beyond the grave.

Our gospel assures the individual that he is known to God and loved by Him. God cannot lightly cast him aside. I, as a father, whose love is broken and imperfect, am prepared to make any sacrifice necessary so that every worthy hope of my child can be fulfilled. How much more will God, whose love is perfect and unbroken, do for His children? Will He allow the longing for eternal life to be stifled and unfulfilled?

John Baille has written of God's love and eternal life for the individual. "But if God is the God of individuals, if individuals can enter into fellowship with Him, if individuals are precious in His sight, then our hope in God necessarily becomes a hope for the individual.

"The argument is unanswerable; and is indeed the only unanswerable argument for immortality that has ever been given, or ever can be given. It cannot be evaded by a denial of the premises. If the individual can commune with God, then he must matter to God. And if he matters to God, he must share God's eternity. For if God really rules, He cannot be conceived as scrapping what is precious in His sight. It is in the conjunction with God that the promise of eternal life resides."[7]

Let the modern preacher know that great preaching has always

---

7. John Baillie, *And the Life Everlasting* (New York: Charles Scribner's Sons, 1933), p. 163

been concerned with individual man; that no man has a more strategic place than the preacher to counteract the growing anonymity of our time; and that no message has greater power to touch the deep springs of life than the gospel. Let him then give serious attention to addressing the gospel to persons. If he will, he need not fear for his pulpit.

11 / PREACHING TO CORPORATE MAN

"NONE OF US LIVES TO HIMSELF, AND NONE OF US DIES TO HIM-self" (Rom. 14:7, RSV). That is as true today as when Paul wrote it. And while Paul's immediate concern was to stress the Lordship of Jesus Christ, whose we are in life and death, the truth suggests a basic human solidarity which is always true of man. Our lives are bound up together. Our lives intersect. We are involved in humanity. Man is corporate as well as individual.

As has already been suggested, the individual and corporate dimensions of life are two of the basic poles of human existence. Both are real. Preaching that neglects either, neglects a basic side of man's life. The preacher must, therefore, address the gospel to corporate man.

The modern preacher should realize that corporate man will continue to grow, not diminish, in our time. Mergers in business and industry will likely continue; smaller political units will be absorbed in larger ones; the complexities of modern life will demand increased social organizations; government will assume an increasing role; and the symbols that interpret modern life will progressively become more impersonal.

Corporate Man

Corporate man is a reality. There is a sense in which man is corporate before he is individual. For example, a person becomes conscious of the you over against him before he becomes aware of the I he is. Without a prior awareness of the you, a person could scarcely become aware of the I in any significant and fulfilling sense.

In the most solitary moment, a person can hear the shuffling of feet. Who goes there? Fellow travelers. There are others who accompany a man on his journey of life. No man ever reaches destination alone. Fellow travelers make meaningful the journey, help define its goal, and help determine the ways and means of reaching destination.

Carson McCullers, in her beautiful little play *The Members of the Wedding* pictures movingly and poignantly the loneliness of a twelve-year-old girl, Frankie. "Shush," she says, "just now I realized something. The trouble with me is that a long time I have been just an 'I' person. All other people say 'we.' When Bernice says 'we,' she means her lodge and church and colored people. Soldiers can say 'we' and mean the army. All people belong to a 'we' except me." Then she began to find new meaning in the sense of belonging with her brother and his bride: "I love the two of them so much that we belong together," she said. "I love the two of them so much because they are the we of me."[1]

There is always the we of me. There are many of these we groups who determine the kind of me I will be. We belong to families, communities, schools, churches, clubs, fellowships, fraternities, intimate social groups, industries, businesses, professions, labor unions, trade associations, professional societies, political parties, social classes, races, and a nation.

Out of these deep and basic relationships comes behavior that is more than personal and individual. It is corporate behavior. Often there is real tension between the individual and the corporate life, personal values and corporate values, personal idealism and corporate realism.

Biblical faith is much more aware of the corporate nature of life than is modern man. While the individual emerges more clearly at certain points of Biblical history than at others, great stress is placed at all times on the corporate life. In the Old Testament, a people is thrown into sharp focus. They are the bearer of God's purpose in history. The Word of God often comes to the nation. The nation, when guilty of sin and apostasy, must repent in

---

1. Carson McCullers, *The Member of the Wedding* (New York: A New Direction Paperback, 1946), pp. 51-52

order to receive God's forgiveness, acceptance, and renewal. When the nation persists in its stubborn rebellion against God, the heavy hand of God's judgment falls upon it.

In the New Testament, there is still the strong corporate emphasis. A new people, the church, emerges. Paul stressed the corporate nature of the church when he compared it to a body. "For just as the body is one and has many members," he wrote, "and all the members of the body, though many, are one body, so it is with Christ. For by one Spirit we were baptized into one body —Jews or Greeks, slaves or free—and all were made to drink of one Spirit" (I Cor. 12:12-13), RSV).

Jesus, in the prayer he gave His followers, stressed the corporate nature of life. Not a single singular first person pronoun is used. They are all plural. God is to be addressed not as *my* Father but *our* Father. The petitions we are to make on our behalf have a strong corporate sense. We ask to be given *our* daily bread, to be forgiven *our* trespasses, and that *we* be delivered from evil.

I remember members of Alcoholic Anonymous closing one of their meetings with the Lord's prayer. I had never heard it said with so much meaning and reality before. I shall never forget the feeling with which they prayed, "Give us . . . forgive us . . . deliver us." They had not been delivered from the evils of alcoholism privately. While their deliverance had a deep personal meaning, hands had reached out to lift them up. They were members of a fellowship of deep identification where they were accepted, understood, and cared for without judgment. Their redemption had a corporate meaning.

The Sin of Corporate Man

We frequently interpret sin in terms that are too individualistic. There is such a thing as corporate guilt. Yet, the individual may be painfully conscious of his guilt, while a political party, an industry, or the nation may feel scarcely any guilt at all. However, the truth is that corporate man is frequently more immoral than individual man. Men will frequently indulge in behavior together which would be repugnant to them personally.

Forty years ago Reinhold Niebuhr wrote a book entitled *Moral Man and Immoral Society*. In this book Niebuhr said that man is more moral than his society. He wrote of how the individual is endowed with sympathy and a sense of justice that society is not blessed with. The individual can refine and purge egotistic elements that society is incapable of doing. He is more able to see a social situation with a greater objectivity and to sacrifice selfish ambition for the common goal than is a social group. He may seek the advantage of others rather than his own. "But all these achievements are more difficult if not impossible," he wrote, "for human societies and social groups. In every human group, there is less reason to guide and check impulse, less capacity for self-transcendence, less ability to comprehend the needs for others and therefore more unrestrained egotism than the individuals, who compose the group, reveal in their personal relationships."[2]

John W. Gardner has pointed up the same truth: "One of the most common phenomena of modern life is the sight of a man of the highest personal values presiding over an institution that mocks those values. Forty years ago Lincoln Steffens noted that some of the most evil political machines he encountered were presided over by men of rather high personal moral standards. Similarly today the television network that merchandises violence may be presided over by a man who personally abhors violence, and the industrial company that spews pollutants into the city's air and water may be run by a man who wouldn't drop a chewing-gum wrapper on the sidewalk."[3]

It takes only a little observation and reflection to realize that man is more moral than his society; that the individual man is normally more idealistic than corporate man.

Reference has already been made to how the most respectable forces of society—the state as the custodian of justice and organized religion as the guardian of faith and morality—joined hands in putting Jesus Christ to death. Possibly no one individual would have been so callous and brutal with Jesus. This is especially illustrated in Pilate. He was personally drawn to Jesus and believed Him to be an innocent man. He wanted to free Him but was eventually overridden by the pressure and demands of the various groups. Pilate was, no doubt, a more morally sensitive man than his official decision indicated.

I remember an American soldier who was killed in Sicily during

2. Reinhold Niebuhr, *Moral Man and Immoral Society* (New York: Charles Scribner's Sons, 1932), pp. *xi, xii*

3. John W. Gardner, *The Recovery of Confidence* (New York: W. W. Norton and Company, Inc., 1970), p. 136

World War II. He was a captain commanding an infantry company, and he lost his life in taking an enemy-held hill. When the graves registration team picked up his body, they found that he was without his helmet. Surviving members of his company told how he discarded his helmet and was out in front of his men, waving them on, as they assaulted the enemy. He had become a fearless leader and a courageous killer. Yet, a subsequent letter from his sister told of how gentle and idealistic he was as a boy. He would not own a gun and he had never so much as killed a bird. There had been strong pacifistic tendencies in his life. He became a professional musician. But as a member of the army he would do things which would have been revolting to him in his personal life.

Sometime ago I visited a predominantly Negro high school. It was there that I realized, more than ever before, how deeply our society has injured and scarred black people. I said to a Negro girl: "You are pretty." And she covered her face with her hands, making no effort to acknowledge the compliment in any positive way. Who had so marred her self-image that she could not accept a compliment? Possibly no individual in our area would have deliberately injured her so deeply. Who did then? Our society. And in our society were many fine people who would have been kind and generous to the girl in personal relationships, but who had allowed the prejudice and discrimination of our corporate life against black people to almost destroy her.

But why is corporate man more immoral and sinful than individual man? Power is concentrated in our corporate structures, and while appealing strongly to the pride and vanity of the group, it is not as easily controlled and directed to humane ends as when it is in personal hands. Decision-making is removed further and further from the individual, and the sense of personal involvement and responsibility suffers. There is not the clearly defined sense of right and wrong in corporate life as in personal living. Moral values are more blurred. People injured by corporate action are often far removed from the place of policy making and, therefore, can appear more as statistics and less as persons.

This can be illustrated by an industry, once locally owned and relatively small, which has been merged with a larger industrial complex. Before the merger, there was a close relationship between management and employees. Following the merger, there was an effort to streamline the industry, making it more efficient and at the same time reducing costs. Men who had been employed for many years were laid off. It was a tragically brutal thing for these men. Policy-making was now farther removed and the personal equation was more and more lost. Those injured could be thought of more as statistics in cost reduction and less as persons. This could be done with much less moral anguish than when the industry was smaller and more personal relationships prevailed.

While corporate man is more immoral than individual man, he does not feel his guilt, as has been observed, as keenly as the individual. It usually takes a dramatically tragic situation to make an institution or society feel its guilt. A nation, for example, is seldom if ever broken and contrite save in defeat. A national tragedy, like the assasination of the late President John F. Kennedy, may stir the conscience of a nation. But the sense of guilt may be shallow and short-lived.

Yet, we must not make the mistake of declaring individual man pure and innocent while making our institutions responsible for the evil and injustice in our world. "Some of today's revolutionaries," writes John W. Gardner, "particularly younger ones, have fallen victim to an old and naive doctrine—that man is naturally good, humane, decent, just, and honorable, but that corrupt and wicked institutions have transformed the noble savage into a civilized monster. Destroy the corrupt institutions, they say, and man's native goodness will flower. There isn't anything in history or anthropology to confirm the thesis, but it has survived down the generations."[4]

The truth is that man builds into his corporate life the selfishness, pride, and lust for power that are already in his heart. And while evil in the corporate life becomes more powerful because, as already suggested, there is a lessening of personal responsibility, a dulling of conscience, a blurring of moral values, and a removing of individuals to greater distances so that faces can more easily become numbers, we must not forget the source of evil. Evil was in man before it was in his society.

Redemption of Corporate Man

Many see redemption only in terms of the individual. Here is a man who says: What we need to do is get the slum out of the man,

4. Ibid., p. 44

not the man out of the slum. When I hear something like that, I want to ask: Why not both?

"In every discussion of a social problem," writes Roger L. Shinn, "somebody sooner or later says, 'The way to get a better world is to get better people,' or, 'The answer to that social problem [war, social tension, disputes between capital and labor] is to change the hearts of men.' By this time in history that judgment has surely been proven wrong. We always need better people and changed hearts. But we also need better institutions to implement human generosity, to thwart human evil, and to channel organizational processes that unintentionally hurt as well as help people."[5]

Redemption, if it is to be Biblical, must be both individual and corporate. The word of God in the Bible is addressed, not only to the individual, but to a nation with its basic institutions. The modern preacher, therefore, must address the gospel to corporate man with his institutions and social behavior. He must be concerned with such social realities as war, poverty, and racism.

If the preacher wants Biblical authority for this, let him look to the Hebrew prophets of the eighth century. Amos, for example, was compelled to speak the word of God to the corporate structures of the society.

Amos blasted the iniquities of the social, economic, and political life of the nation. The strong exploited the weak, and the rich profited from the poor. ". . . they sell the righteous for silver, and the needy for a pair of shoes—they that trample the head of the poor into the dust of the earth, and turn aside the way of the afflicted" (Amos 2:6-7, RSV). Judges could be easily bribed, and justice miscarried in the courts. And Amos did not spare the sanctuaries and organized religion.

Popular religion felt comfortable with social injustice. They flourished side by side. Hands that brought costly gifts to the altar frequently had cheated and stolen in the market place. Worship all too frequently, rather than stabbing the people awake to social iniquities, lulled them to sleep and salved their guilty consciences. The people believed that going through the formalities of worship would cause God to overlook their dishonesty, exploitation, and political graft. But the prophet warned them: Worship that does

---

5. Roger L. Shinn, *Tangled World* (New York: Charles Scribner's Sons, 1965), p. 58

not issue in social justice and compassion is not acceptable to God. The modern preacher must preach the Word of God to a much more complicated society than the eighth-century Hebrew prophet. There is a strange blending of good and evil in our modern technological society. Therefore, the word of judgment spoken by the preacher must be more than the blind blasting of his society.

There are forces in our society that are depersonalizing, devitalizing, and dehumanizing. The individual is frequently in danger of losing his identity and in some cases is more expendable than the machine. There is discrimination and injustice in our society. The word of judgment must be spoken against these. But there is good in our society that needs to be supported and encouraged.

The perforations on an IBM card may be a symbol of depersonalization. But the organization that uses this card may experience moral gains. Corporations have worked out humane plans for sick leave and health insurance for their employees. The corporation may fulfill the Biblical injunction to bear one another's burden as the cost of individual sickness is distributed throughout the organization. As Roger Shinn has suggested, "cooperation, as truly as individualism, has moral value. It is not clear that the old-fashioned rugged individualist, who eyed every man as a competitor, had richer human relations than the modern man, who must work with many others in an organization."[6]

When the word of judgment has been spoken, as it must be, the preacher should realize that beyond that word there is the possibility of a new direction, renewal, and redemption for the corporate life.

When I speak of redemption, I do not use the term in an absolute sense. By redemption, I mean that our institutions can become more just, our corporate life more moral, and our society more humane. This redemption has a theological meaning in that God's grace works in the corporate structures of our world and our institutions can be God's instrument for fulfilling his purpose in history.

Jesus preached the coming of the Kingdom of God, and taught us to pray for its coming. He did this in the assurance that when we preach or pray for the coming of the Kingdom of God we are doing more than indulging in wishful thinking. We are grappling

---

6. Ibid., p. 55

with reality. Whenever and wherever the Kingdom of God is coming, corporate life is being redeemed. And while preaching to the corporate life is a hard task, we dare not turn from it. We have been commissioned to confront corporate man with the claims of God.

12 / PREACHING THE FULL GOSPEL TO THE WHOLE MAN

WE OFTEN PREACH A FRAGMENTED GOSPEL. THIS IS TO BE UNFAIR to the message we preach. We frequently address the gospel to only a part of man. This is to be unfaithful to those to whom we preach. God is concerned about the whole person in his total setting, and God would redeem the whole life. We are called upon to preach the full gospel to the whole man. In so doing lies the direction, in part at least, toward the recovery of the pulpit in our time.

The Full Gospel

A symbol of the full gospel is the Bible on our pulpits, containing the Old and New Testaments. These cannot be separated. The New Testament emerged from the living background of the Old, and the Old Testament is fulfilled in the New.

We are to preach the full Biblical revelation as we have received it through the history, law, poetry, prophets, gospels, letters and apocalypses of the Bible.

We must preach the God of the whole Bible. In the Old Testament He is seen a little differently than in the New Testament, but He is the same God with the same unfailing purpose. The God of the Old Testament is a God of power, law, and justice. Yet He is not without mercy and grace. "He does not deal with us according to our sins, nor requite us according to our iniquities. For as the heavens are high above the earth, so great is his steadfast love toward those who fear him; as far as the east is from the west, so far does he remove our transgressions from us" (Ps. 103:10-11,

RSV). In the New Testament, God is revealed essentially as a God of love and grace, yet he is not without law and justice. He is the God who ". . . now commands all men everywhere to repent, because He has fixed a day on which He will judge the world in righteousness by a man whom He has appointed . . ." (Acts 17:30-31, RSV). Jesus Christ has stripped away the veil so God can be seen in a clearer light. But He is the God whom we have met in the Old Testament.

We preach the God of the Bible as a trinity—God the Father and Creator above us, God the Son in our history, and God the Holy Spirit present with us. We should remember, as we preach God as trinity, that the Trinity was experience before it was doctrine. The doctrine is an attempt to give a rational account of the experience. In the New Testament, this doctrine of the Trinity is beginning to take shape, but it is more experience there than dogma. It has the feel of life about it. We must still preach the Trinity as the way men experience God rather than as cold, abstract dogma. Yet, we must be prepared to answer the searching questions that will be asked about it. An intelligible explanation will always be necessary. We cannot escape the task of theology. God has created our world with its life; therefore, our existence has purpose and meaning. The greatness of God can be seen in His act of creation. He spoke and creation happened. The psalmist could speak of the heavens as the work of God's fingers (Ps. 8:3). He was writing poetry and expressing an idea artistically. But He was doing more. Creation was no burden. God did it with the light touch of His fingers. In the creation story as told in the first chapter of Genesis, the author in speaking of God creating the heavens, said: "He made the stars also" (Gen. 1:16). The creating of the stars was almost an afterthought. To speak of such a God is to speak of wonder and mystery which are the sources of worship.

The world which God has created is a real world and the cradle of man's history. Man's history is real, crucial, and tragic. God is concerned about man, and has entered man's history in a strange, new and unique way. God entered man's history through the door nearest and most congenial to him, which was a person since God is personal. He entered it in His Son, Jesus Christ, to redeem man. That is what makes the gospel good news. Therefore, Jesus Christ is the focus of our preaching. As earlier suggested, we preach Jesus Christ in His birth, life, death, resurrection, ascension, His position at the right hand of the Father, which is the place of sovereign power, and His future return to consummate man's long and tedious years.

It is not enough, however, to preach God the Father and Creator who is above us, nor God the Son in some remote age of our history. God is present with us in the person of the Holy Spirit. God is not only above His creation. He is within it. The psalmist could ask: "Whither shall I go from thy Spirit? Or whither shall I flee from thy presence?" (Ps. 139:7, RSV). There was no place in God's creation where he could escape the presence of God. In the New Testament, there is a greater, sharper, and more clearly defined emphasis on the Holy Spirit. The reason for this is that the Holy Spirit is seen in the light of the historic Jesus as well as the source of strength that vitalizes the church.

We preach the God of the Bible as engaging in an alternating action with man. He deals with man in terms of judgment and mercy. C. H. Dodd speaks of this as God's "two-beat rhythm." God's judgment is more than moral laws with which man collides and upon which he bruises and destroys himself. God sets his face against evil. God opposes the arrogant, proud, and evil action of man. His judgment is severe, like the blasting winds from the desert. Therefore, man dare not think sentimentally about God as if He were a benign cosmic grandfather.

Yet, God deals with man in great mercy and grace. When man turns from evil, God accepts, restores, and forgives him. His mercy reaches to the uttermost and His grace descends into the deepest despair.

A special people, called by God for a redemptive purpose in history, is a part of the full gospel. In the Old Testament, it is Israel; in the New Testament, it is the new Israel or the church. There is a continuity between the two, and the church cannot be understood apart from Israel. Men from all nations, races, and classes are called into its fellowship. And Jesus Christ, who was the promise of Israel, stands at the center of the church's life as the great reality. The church, just as Israel, is uniquely related to God in a covenant relationship.

The church is many faceted, as has already been observed, and many metaphors are used in the New Testament to describe it. But we come near to its basic nature when we think of the church as the people of God.

One of the great temptations of preachers is not to preach the full gospel. We pick and choose those parts that are congenial to our temperament, theological position, and church. When we do this, we preach a fragmented and broken gospel.

I remember seeing Thomas Jefferson's New Testament. Jefferson was a deist who believed that God had created the world only to abandon it, leaving it to its own laws and momentum. There was no place for miracles in our world or the intervention of God in human affairs. Therefore, Jefferson had deleted events that told of the supernatural and miraculous. I was shocked! Why would anyone be so irreverent and arrogant as to handle God's word in such a manner? But I now know that most of us do that kind of thing. It is true that we would not tear pages from the Bible, but we mutilate it in much more subtle ways. Some of the most multilated Bibles I have ever seen have been in the hands of men who avowed a passionate love of the Bible and claimed to believe every word of it. Mentally, they had ripped great sections from it and were blind to many of its great truths.

The fragmentation of the Biblical revelation is the source of heresy. Heresy is not an untruth. Heresy is a truth overly accented, lifted from context, or isolated from other inseparable truths. And heresy is an attractive truth, speaking to some deep need. Otherwise, it would not be so widely accepted. We know the historic heresies of the church, but we may preach contemporary heresies and not be aware of them.

The Whole Man

Preaching is proclaiming the gospel to men. But as already observed, we must be careful to preach the full gospel. And we must be just as careful to address it to the whole man.

Man is not divided into body and soul. He is a unit and a whole, a very complex being. The gospel is addressed to the whole man because God intends to redeem the whole life. Yet, often it is said, "The purpose of the church is to get souls saved." And there is an obvious and important truth in the claim. But it is truth that has neglected other important and inseparable truths. It is, therefore, one of the popular heresies of our time. A moment of reflection will allow us to remember that the Bible does not talk that way. The cleverest prooftexter would find it difficult to find even a narrow Biblical basis of support for such a view. The rationale for the claim is that the soul is immortal and therefore the most important part of a man's life. But this is more Greek thinking than Christian faith. The Greek mind envisioned salvation in terms of the soul being delivered from the body which was its prison. Christian faith, on the other hand, envisions, not only the soul, but the whole life being saved. The body is to be redeemed ultimately. "This mortal must put on immortality." We are to be given new bodies befitting the new order.

The disciples were to be fishers, not merely of souls, but of men. Jesus Christ did not say that he came just to save souls. He came that men might have life more abundantly.

Man is involved in basic relationship. While there will be an intellectual, emotional, volitional, and spiritual response to the gospel, the gospel will not be addressed to the mind, heart, will, and soul as abstract qualities of man. The gospel is to be preached to man in his wholeness as he is involved in these primary relationships. What are these relationships?

First, the gospel is addressed to man in his relationship with God.

The great tragedy of his life is that he is separated from God. Man is a sinner. The essence of his sin is not breaking laws, but pride that removes God from the center of his life, putting self there. Therefore, man is cut off from the basic source of his life which is God. He is lonely, anxious, insecure. He is burdened with guilt, and meaninglessness, like a dark night, settles over him. Man is lost. He needs forgiveness and reconciliation with God.

The good news of the gospel is that God, while taking man's sin seriously, loves him in his rebellion and seeks him in his lostness. God takes the initiative in setting things right. The chasm that separates man from God has been spanned from God's side, and God has crossed over to stand in the midst of man's broken and alien life. Man, therefore, need not live like an alien, held captive by dark powers that would destroy him. He can now return to the One whose he is, the Father who loves and cares for him.

A man comes to God with empty hands. He has nothing with which to commend himself to God, and he has no moral coinage with which to buy God's favor. But the wonder of it all is that he needs nothing. God looks at our empty hands with mercy and assures us that His salvation is a gift. It is of grace.

God is like the father in Jesus' story of the Prodigal Son, looking at his profligate boy who was penniless, dressed in tattered rags, without a ring and sandals. The boy had nothing with which to buy a new outfit. But he needed nothing. The father clothed his son with the best from his wardrobe, free and without cost to the boy. Then he had a banquet in honor of the boy's homecoming. And the father, in joy and pride, said to the guests, "This is my son."

Second, the gospel is addressed to man in relation to his brother. The gospel has, not only a personal, but a social dimension.

The good news of the gospel is, as we have already observed, that a man does not have to be lost and alienated from God. He can be God's son. But it does not stop there. He does not have to be the enemy of his brother. He can be his brother's brother. At the heart of our gospel is reconciliation that is two-dimensional. Man can be reconciled to God *and* man. Biblical faith knows nothing of one kind of reconciliation without the other. They are two sides of one reality and can no more be separated than can the back and palm of a hand.

R. B. Y. Scott has said: "One of the most notable and original features of the teachings of the Hebrew prophets is their repeated insistence that the Lord is more concerned with men's behavior in their social relationships than with formal worship offered."[1] The conclusion is inescapable when you hear Amos say, "Take away from me the noise of your songs; to the melody of your harps I will not listen. But let justice roll down like waters, and righteousness like an overflowing stream" (Amos 5:23-24, RSV); or Micah: "He has showed you, O man, what is good; and what does the Lord require of you but to do justice, and to love kindness, and to walk humbly with your God?" (Micah 6:8, RSV).

There can be no doubt that Jesus followed in the prophetic tradition. In Jesus' inaugural announcement before the congregation He knew so well at Nazareth, He said he had come to proclaim the acceptable year of the Lord, to preach the gospel to the poor, to release captives, restore sight to the blind, and give liberty to the oppressed (Luke 4:16-20). His ministry unfolded in that pattern. He was concerned that the religionists of his time had neglected the weightier matters of the law, "justice and mercy and faith" (Matt. 23:23, RSV).

"Get a man's heart right and everything else will be right." How

---

1. R. B. Y. Scott, *The Interpreter's Bible* (Nashville: Abingdon Press, 1951, Vol. 5), p. 170

often we have heard that. Once more there is a great truth here. Men's hearts can be changed. Without that the gospel would not be good news. But it is truth lifted out of a wider context of truth. It does not follow that everything else will automatically be right when a man's heart is changed. The changed heart needs the most rigorous ethical and social discipline. Jesus obviously felt that way. He said a man must be so radically changed at the center of his life that the experience could be spoken of as a new birth. But He also gave the Sermon on the Mount, which is the world's finest ethical teaching.

Paul said that if any man be in Christ, he is a new creation. But he also stressed the great ethical and social demands of the Christian faith. In some of his epistles, like Romans and Ephesians, the first part is given to theology while the second part is devoted to ethics and social responsibility. Where the division is not made so clearly, Paul's letters are like tapestries with faith and ethics being interwoven.

Third, the gospel is addressed to man in relation to his world.

God created the world. Upon completing creation, God placed staggering responsibilities in man's hands. Man was to have dominion over nature (Gen. 1:28). The psalmist could say: "Thou hast given him dominion over the works of thy hands; thou hast put all things under his feet" (Ps. 8:6, RSV). God is creator and therefore owner. Man is master but his responsibility is that of a steward.

While being given dominion over the earth, man is dependent upon it. He has been created from the dust. His life is grounded in the earth. The chemistry of his body is that of the soil. Earth is his mother. She nurtures and keeps him. In her his life is cradled, and she is the stage upon which his history unfolds. His life, with its health, happiness, and fulfillment, is inextricably involved with the physical world. Love nature, and he loves himself. Protect nature and he protects himself. Destroy nature and he destroys himself.

Man has been a poor steward of his earth. He has frequently stripped her of her beauty and left her naked and ugly. He has often exploited her wealth and given back to her his refuse and waste. He has widely polluted the air, made unclean the streams, and poisoned the soil. He has made nature sick and now she threatens to disgorge him. It is as if nature, now made angry, raises her hand to strike down man.

An environmental crisis is on us. Life on our planet is threatened. If a catastrophe of such proportions should overtake us, white and black, educated and illiterate, rich and poor would perish together. The environmental crisis may be the most serious we face.

We have said that it is sinful to break God's laws and injure people who are His children. Now we must say that it is sinful to injure God's creation. It is sinful to exploit nature, rob her of her wealth, and make her sick with our refuse.

We must call men to take seriously his stewardship of nature. Man must protect and love her. He must guard her wealth and replenish her where he has taken from her. He must make her more productive and enhance her beauty. He must make pure her air, clean her streams, and sweet her soil. He must care for the earth which has given him physical birth, nurtured his physical life, and created the stage upon which his history is fulfilled.

The task is laid on us! We must preach the full gospel to the whole man. To fail here, is to fail our message, the people to whom we preach, ourselves, and God.

13 / PREACHING TO MEN OF POWER

No man in history has held such tremendous power as modern man. Increasingly he pushes his dominion from one area of existence to another, ranging from genes, which are the bearers of life qualities, to cosmic space. We speak of genetic engineering and space technology. The modern preacher should know, therefore, if he is to preach at all, he must preach to men of power.

Can the gospel speak to the spectacle of power in our modern world? While power as such is amoral, can the gospel enable man to become more moral so he can handle his power responsibly? Does it have the power to transform men and their society? Or is the gospel too spiritual, idealistic, and other worldly for our hard world where power is often impersonal and ruthless? Is our gospel out of place, a stranger in our kind of world?

One thing is obvious. If the preacher is to catch the attention of our generation and influence it, he must preach a gospel of power. If he cannot, he will be uncertain, defensive, and apologetic about his task. He will feel that he is a pygmy preaching to giants.

The New Testament makes a staggering claim for the gospel: It is the power of God unto salvation. The preacher must believe this if he is to be effective. He must believe that the gospel has the power to redeem man, make him more moral, and give him a greater social awareness. If it can't why preach?

A Gospel of Power

Paul in writing his letter to the church at Rome, said, "For I

am not ashamed of the gospel: it is the power of God for salvation
to everyone who has faith, to the Jew first and also to the Greek"
(Rom. 1:16, RSV).

Rome was the center of world power. She was the capital of the
civilized world that centered around the Mediterranean Sea. Rome
ruled that world through an elaborate political and judicial system.
The remotest province felt Roman rule and justice. Roman legions
kept peace in that world, and a vast system of highways had Rome
as their hub. Revenue from all over the world made rich her
treasuries. Here was power as the world has rarely seen it. Paul,
anticipating a visit to that imperial city, spoke of the gospel as
being the power of God. He used the language Rome best understood when he spoke of the gospel as power. He would not, therefore, be timid and apologetic. He would go armed with confidence.

The test of the power of the gospel was its ability to change
men. Could lives be transformed by the gospel? Paul answered that
question like this: "Therefore, if anyone is in Christ, he is a new
creation; the old has passed away, behold, the new has come"
(II Cor. 5:17, RSV).

This was not theory and speculation with Paul. His life had
been changed, and there was nothing he knew so well as that.
Christ had turned him around, giving him a new center of loyalty
and a new scale of values. He had a new life under a new Lord.
That which he once loved, he now rejected; and that which he
once hated, he now loved.

James Reid, in commenting on the possibility of a man being
a new creation in Christ, has said, "He is not merely improved, or
reformed, or altered in any way which implies no more than an
external change, however great; he is remade. He is different even
from what he was at his best. His change is radical; it goes to the
root of his being."[1]

So men in every generation have borne witness that life can be
radically changed by Jesus Christ.

John Newton was an outstanding English preacher and hymn
writer of the eighteenth century. As a young man, he had lived a
very reckless and profligate life. He joined the English navy, and,
after deserting it, engaged in the slave trade. During a storm at sea,
he was converted. Remembering that experience when his life was

1. James Reid, *The Interpreter's Bible,* Vol. 10 (New York and Nashville:
Abingdon-Cokesbury Press, 1953), p. 338

changed, he said, "I can never forget two things: first, that I was a great sinner; and second, that Jesus is a great saviour." He wrote his own epitaph:

> *John Newton, clerk,*
> *once an infidel and libertine,*
> *a servant of slaves in Africa,*
> *was by the rich mercy of our Lord and Saviour,*
> *Jesus Christ,*
> *preserved, restored, pardoned*
> *and appointed to preach the faith he*
> *had laboured to destroy.*

All testimonies to the power of Jesus Christ to redeem life are not as dramatic as those of Paul and Newton. Many bear their witness in ways less dramatic, but no less certain, that Jesus has made the great difference in their lives. He has reconciled them to God and their fellows, giving them a new purpose, peace, and power.

But the power of Christ to transform life goes beyond the individual. The gospel can change social relationships and social structures. This can be easily overlooked. We must not forget that Jesus crashed social barriers and violated social proprieties to get to the socially alienated and the untouchables of His day. He was the friend of publicans and sinners and ate with them. It was His social action more than His theological ideas that got Him into trouble. From His brave example have gone forth healing and reconciling forces that are active in our world to this day.

It is often said that Paul left the social structures of his time, even the worst ones, untouched. He seemed to accept them with an easy conscience. He did not, for example, condemn slavery but urged the slave to be obedient to his master. What is often forgotten is that it takes numbers and political power to change social structures, and the first generation of Christians had neither. So, rather than making a frontal attack on social evils, their approach was more subtle and indirect. When Paul told Philemon to accept Onesimus, his run-away slave, as no longer a slave but a beloved brother, he announced a principle that one day would help destroy slavery.

But why does the gospel have the kind of power the New Testament speaks about? Because love is the ultimate power. This is so since God is love. God so loved the world that He gave His only begotten Son, and through Jesus Christ, the Son of God, the love of God has entered our world like a healing stream. Jesus' new commandment was that His followers should love one another as He had loved them, and His disciples would be identified down the ages by their love one for another. Paul said that love never fails.

Imagine a mushrooming cloud rising above a fated city where an atom bomb has been dropped. Then strange configurations begin to appear in the cloud, one of them a lamb. How odd and unusual, we would say. The lamb, a symbol of gentleness, meekness, even weakness, would seem so out of place in the midst of such power.

Yet, there is even a stranger scene in the fifth chapter of Revelation. A slain lamb is seen in the midst of the throne of God, the place of sovereign power. The lamb seems so out of place until we remember that it represents Jesus Christ through whom the love of God has had free access into our broken world. And then we know that He is not out of place, since only love is really strong.

We remember Jesus on that first Good Friday. We see Him standing alone with no one to defend Him in the court. And He attempted no defense for Himself. He stumbled beneath His cross through the streets of the city, lined with jeering crowds, and was put to death on the cross He carried. He seemed so weak and helpless. But history knows now that He alone was strong on that fateful day.

Jesus knew that men strut, display power, and court pomp and ceremony in order to conceal weakness. He dared to appear weak and helpless knowing that He was strong. The strength of the eternal God was in Him.

Man of Power

Modern man progressively extends his control over the vitalities of his own life and the universe around him.

The new biology and chemistry have given man remarkable power over his own life. We are all familiar with organ transplants and "miracle" drugs. We now have drugs that greatly affect the emotional, mental, and psychic functions of man. It has been proven that there is an intimate relation between electronic and behavioral aspects of animal life and presumably in man, too. But man will find his greatest power over his own life in his ability to use genes, the bearer of hereditary traits, in desired ways.

Some scientists recommend the establishment of sperm banks, for the maintenance, in a frozen state, of the semen of distinguished men. These men could become, through artificial insemination, the genetic fathers of many persons. The immediate result would be greatly improved persons, and the ultimate end, some believe, might be the appearance of a kind of superman.

But beyond a selective control over the use of genes, scientists can now change the molecular structure of genes. This opens up possibilities that are awesome. It may be that man can control his own life and future in a way never dreamed of before. Some believe that scientists are now ready to produce a new kind of man who could be infinitely better or worse than anything we have known. It all depends on who controls the genes. This poses terrifying ethical problems. Roger L. Shinn wonders if there will be a genetic race, comparable to the armaments race, as nations compete to develop superwarriors for the future.[2]

Man also moves rapidly in extending his control over his physical universe. He progressively eliminates the barriers of distance and time, overcomes famine and disease, and conquers cosmic space.

Nowhere is man's inventive genius more clearly seen than in his production of thinking machines. Some scientists believe that within a decade we shall develop a machine with the general intelligence of an average human being. Such a machine will read a book, tell a joke, perform a kind deed, or have a fight. But what is more astounding, this machine is expected to have powers of self-improvement. By educating itself, the machine will attain genius level and develop incalculable powers.

Today's nuclear bomb is many times more powerful than the one dropped on Hiroshima. Whole nations could be paralyzed within a few minutes in a nuclear war and ultimately destroyed. We no longer speak of Russia and the United States, the two powers having the great arsenals of nuclear power, as being able merely to kill each other's population. We speak of the overkill. They can now overkill each other several times.

Modern man seems ready to take into his hands the mystery

---

2. Robert L. Shinn, *Man: The New Humanism*, Vol. VI, New Directions in Theology Today (Philadelphia: The Westminster Press, 1968), p. 80

of life. We have seen man's dazzling strides in the exploration of his own life and the conquest of his world, but the mystery of life has eluded him. God has kept the creation of life for himself, we have said. Now we would not be surprised to see bold headlines across the front page of our newspaper announcing the creation of life in some laboratory of our world. We expect it. When it happens, it will be simple and rudimentary, but it will be life. Thus man will be handling the mystery we thought belonged to God alone.

An increasing number of scientists and a knowledge explosion have made possible this immense power. Half of the scientists of all time are alive today. Ninety percent of all the information ever developed in the physical and biological sciences has been developed since 1940. This scientific knowledge is doubling every seven years, and within the near future will be doubling every three or four years. So we wonder if we shall be able to assimilate the power that will be thrust upon us.

Man is frightened by his power. He is afraid he doesn't have sufficient moral strength to control it, manage it responsibly, and direct it to humane ends. He is better at conquering his physical universe than mastering himself. He has developed his scientific instruments more rapidly than he improved himself. He is better at exploring space than building human relations. His scientific advance has outdistanced his moral progress. And often he has allowed his scientific knowledge and power to replace reverence, mystery, and wonder in his life.

Lesslie Newbigin tells about a conversation he had with a man who was a member of the team of physicists in Chicago who worked on the first atom bomb during the final years of World War II. The scientist told of the mounting excitement as they neared the completion of their project. Then he told of the feeling that came over the whole team when they had succeeded. They were frightened when they realized they had created what could be the most monstrous evil the mind of man had ever conceived and brought forth. Then Newbigin continues with an insightful observation: "Alongside of, or perhaps underneath, the sense of mastery, the assurance that we are only at the beginning of the developments made possible by modern techniques, there is also a sense of something like meaninglessness or even terror as man faces his future. This at least seems to me to be true of the most developed societies. One does not need to be a genius to notice that the suicide rate varies from nation to nation in something like a direct ratio to what is called development."[3]

The thing that accelerated the development of the atom bomb more than anything else was the fear that Germany might produce it first. Albert Einstein, upon learning that the Germans would not succeed in constructing the atom bomb, said he would not have lifted a finger in the effort if he had known Germany was so far behind. He was frightened by what he had helped to produce.

In the lunar orbital flight during Christmas of 1968, our astronauts, 240,000 miles from earth, saw our planet as a small disc in space. Frank Borman said he felt as if he were an ambassador to the larger universe. He wished that he could announce to the universe that earth was at peace, but he could not. He knew it was easier to put men into orbital flight around the moon than for men to live like brothers on earth. Space technology had outdistanced human relationships.

So modern man, with all his knowledge and power, is uneasy, unsure, even frightened. He knows something of crucial importance is missing. He finds it difficult to achieve that which he knows he must if he is to survive with any kind of sanity and decency.

New Men for the New Age

Ours is a new age. It has new speed, new power, new frontiers, new values, new dangers and new opportunities, new fears and new hopes. Part of our problem is that we remain old men in our new world. We need a new moral sensibility. Yet we cling to our old immoralities. We need a new openness to man as man, but we hold on to our class and racial prejudices. We need a broader world outlook, but we walk in our provincial ways. We need a new dedication to community, but we pursue our selfish, individualistic ways. We need to identify with the pain and brokenness of our world, but we hold ourselves aloof, keeping a safe distance lest we get hurt. We need to make our institutions more humane, but, seeing them as centers of vested interest, we are slow to change them. We need a new awareness of spiritual reality, but we squeeze our materialistic values.

The great task of the modern preacher is to confront the men

3. Lesslie Newbigin, *Honest Religion for Secular Man* (London: SCM Press Ltd., 1966), p. 31

of power with the claims of the gospel of power so that they may
be transformed, becoming new men for the new age. Unless he
can preach with the confidence that our gospel can create new
men, he can scarcely afford to waste his time in the pulpit. But can
he have that confidence? I think so.

Preaching is declaring God's saving action in Jesus Christ who
was the embodiment of God's love in our world. But preaching is
more than announcing redemptive acts in the historical past, although you can't have preaching without such proclamation. The
sermon is a vehicle of God's redemptive action now. The past
redemptive action of God in Jesus Christ is extended into the
present moment. The Holy Spirit makes the words of the sermon
the living word of power and redemption. The sermon as redemptive action has been called sacramental preaching, and it has a
firm Biblical basis.

On the Day of Pentecost Peter preached with mighty power.
He had historical perspective. Jesus Christ had come from King
David's line. Peter recalled the life, death, and resurrection of
Jesus. This historical action was in the immediate past, held in the
living memory of those who heard. But the sermon was more than
recalling historical events; it mattered not how immediate, dramatic,
and powerful they were. The sermon was a part of God's saving
action. The redemptive past was projected into the present moment.
The God who had acted so mightily in Jesus Christ found in
Peter's sermon an instrument of redemption. The Holy Spirit was
present making the words of the blundering fisherman the word
of God, powerful to save. Peter's sermon was more than a spoken
discourse. It was an instrument of salvation.

We have referred to Paul's speaking of the gospel as the power
of God unto salvation. Paul obviously meant the gospel as preached,
since in the preceding verse he said, "I am ready to preach the
gospel to you that are at Rome also" (Rom. 1:15). The same God
who had acted mightily in the life, death, and resurrection of Jesus
Christ would be active redemptively in the gospel that was preached.

P. T. Forsyth has written: "To be effective our preaching must
be sacramental. It must be an act of prolonging the Great Act,
mediating it, and conveying it."[4]

Donald Miller who has been greatly influenced by Forsyth says,

_____

4. Op. cit., p. 84

"True preaching is an extension of the Incarnation into the contemporary moment, the transfiguration of the cross and Resurrection from ancient facts of a remote past into living realities of the present. A sermon is an act wherein the crucified, risen Lord personally confronts men either to save or judge them."[5]

John Knox states the same idea this way: "But true preaching is also God's gift to us. It is even more than that; it is God actually giving himself to us."[6]

Therefore, the preacher can feel that his preaching has a double undergirding with power: He proclaims God's mighty, saving action in Jesus Christ, and God acts redemptively in the preaching itself. He may expect new men to be the results of his preaching.

From a friend in Japan in 1968 I had a letter in which he told of meeting Mitsuo Fuchida. "Faye and I had a real treat this past week," he wrote, "as we heard Mr. Mitsuo Fuchida speak, the Japanese commander who led 360 bombers against Pearl Harbor on that fateful day, December 7, 1941. Mr. Fuchida is now a Christian preacher with a glowing testimony of how the Lord changed his life from hatred with a desire for revenge against the Americans to one of peace and love for all people."

Our gospel has that kind of power. Men in our time can become new creations in Christ.

We can, therefore, preach with the same kind of confidence that Robert J. McCracken spoke of: "And the thing to remember is what makes Christianity a Gospel, a piece of great good news, is that it maintains that once man has escaped from the prison of his self-sufficiency the door is open for the inrush of a new power, a power not his own which makes for righteousness. What makes Christianity a Gospel is its affirmation that neither man nor society need stay the way they are. Human nature can be changed. Alongside of education and legislation it sets another watchword, its distinctive watchword regeneration. If Christianity affirms anything at all, it is that human nature can be changed, genuinely, radically and permanently changed."[7]

As we go into our pulpits, we need not feel dwarfed by men of

---

5. Donald G. Miller, *Fire in Thy Mouth* (New York and Nashville, Abingdon Press, 1954), p. 17

6. Op. cit., p. 86

7. Robert J. McCracken, "Christianity in an Atomic Age," *Baptist World Alliance, Eighth Congress* (Philadelphia: The Judson Press, 1950), p. 37

power. While we go not arrogantly, we can go confidently. We can have the assurance that we speak about the greatest power ever known to man, and that that power can change man at the very center of his life and redeem his society to a greater justice and humaneness.

14

PREACHING TO SECULAR MAN

THE MODERN PREACHER, IN DEFINING HIS TASK, MUST CONSIDER secular man. He cannot escape this fact: If he is to preach, he must preach to secular man. He has no other choice. Even the faithful and devout within the church, although they may use traditional religious language, have had their values and feeling about life shaped strongly by secularity.

I use the term secularity in two senses. First, secularity declares a freedom from religious authority and institutions and seeks to establish autonomy in the various spheres of life. Second, secularity looks to no dimension above man, his world, and his history. Man has no resource to draw upon beyond himself. The universe is but the extension of the natural order almost to infinity.

The Reality of Secularity

The overwhelming reality of our day is secularity. "The most significant fact about the time in which we are living," writes Lesslie Newbigin, "is that it is a time in which a single movement of secularization is bringing the peoples of all continents into its sweep."[1]

Secularists are not only to be found among the philosophers, historians, scientists, and sophisticated, but among the masses of people. Secularists "are to be found most of all among the people who make no claim to be intellectuals of any kind, among the great mass of our population, who have been conditioned, by the

---

1. Op. cit., p. 11

gigantic achievements of scientific technology, to accept the world as simply so much raw material for human enjoyment and exploitation, without any consideration of its ultimate basis and source."[2]

The reality of secularity transcends the barriers of culture, nationality, geography, even religion. Men everywhere have a growing sense of a single history, a common destiny.

Men and women in remote villages of the world sit around their radios and hear what is going on in New York, London, Moscow, and Tokyo. They don't feel so remote anymore, and they dare hope that some of the blessings of these great centers of science, culture, and commerce will one day be theirs.

An American met a shepherd in Pakistan. He wore his simple shepherd's garb and had his shepherd's staff, tending his sheep as had his fathers for centuries. But there was something different about this shepherd: he had a transistor radio. He was not only a part of a long, unchanging past. He was tuned into the modern, dynamic, changing world and he felt a part of it.

Secularity is not an unmixed blessing. There are both hope and fear in it. Yet, while fear casts a shadow over man's future, hope seems to be the predominant mood. In many parts of the world, men have seen history as static, and dared to hope for nothing better than their fathers had known. But that is now changed. History is not a revolving door, going round and round. History is dynamic, open-ended, going somewhere. Men now know they can have it better than their fathers ever dreamed. Men bring great expectation to the future. They look with great hope, not only to the achievements of science and technology, but to the realization of human rights, human dignity, and social justice. Modern man, if he does not muff his chance, can come upon unprecedented and unimaginable achievements.

Secularity is with us to stay. It sets its face to the future. It is irreversible. At the international missionary conference of Jerusalem in 1928, secularity (the conference used the term "secularism") was not only listed among the rivals of Christianity such as Hinduism and Islam but was considered to be the greatest of them. At the international missionary conference held at Mexico City, 1963, which was a linear successor of the Jerusalem conference, secularity was spoken of in a different accent. The conference

---

2. E. L. Mascall, *The Secularization of Christianity* (London: Darton, Longman and Todd, 1965), p. 192

spoke of the process, in its main lines, as being irreversible, and recognized that it opened up possibilities of new liberation as well as new forms of servitude for men. Therefore, it becomes our duty to understand secularity in the light of Biblical faith.

Since secularity is with us to stay, the modern preacher must be very conscious of the task of communicating the gospel to secular man. As suggested by Theodore O. Wedel, we have to be aware of, maybe even begin with, the questions he is asking: "How can I find a gracious neighbor? How can we live with one another— husband with wife, parents with children, employer with employee?" Then Wedel continues: "This descent, as it were, to the horizontal plane may prove to be dangerous business . . . but if we trust fully the good news of the Incarnation we shall not be alone on the horizontal plane. Christ will be with us."[3]

Points of Contact

Secularity is not a complete stranger to Biblical faith and the Christian gospel. Indeed, they have much in common. Secularity is often a secularized version of Biblical faith. The modern preacher has a point of contact with secular man as he preaches to him. Let us make four observations.

First, the Bible, in some real sense, is a secular book. "Whatever else it may be, the Bible is a secular book dealing with the sort of events which a news editor accepts for publication in a daily newspaper; it is concerned with secular events, wars, revolutions, enslavements and liberations, migrants, and refugees, famines and epidemics and all the rest. It deals with events which happened and tells a story which can be checked—and is being checked—by the work of archaeologists and historians."[4]

The God of the Bible is often found in secular situations. Jacob encountered God in a wilderness where he had slept on a stone for a pillow. Moses was addressed by God on the backside of a desert. Both were far from altars and chanting priests.

The decisive event of the Old Testament was the deliverance of helpless slaves into freedom. It didn't take place in a temple but at the Red Sea, upon which barges of cargo sailed and which was skirted by caravan routes. It was there that God revealed himself as the great liberator. But you do not hear the intoning of a

3. Op. cit., p. 42
4. Op. cit., p. 20

religious service. You hear the cries of a people about to be set free, the cadence of marching feet, the rumbling of chariot wheels, and the shouting commands of cavalry officers.

The Jews came to their highest and clearest understanding of God far away from their holy soil and temple. They found God by the rivers of Babylon where they could not sing the Lord's song. Nostalgically they remembered their holy city, Jerusalem, that lay in ruins, and their temple that lay in shambles. Where they were they had no holy place or holy of holies. Yet in that land, so barren of religious symbols and meaning, God bade them seek him while he could be found and call upon him while he was near. There they really learned that God is the Lord of the universe and all peoples, who could not be confined to holy places, holy times, and holy men, but who could be found anywhere by common men when they seek God with all their heart.

You feel a secular spirit in the New Testament. Jesus was seen more as a secular man than a holy man. He was more a carpenter than a priest. He called His disciples from secular settings rather than from theological classrooms. They were laymen rather than men who had taken vows of ordination. The setting of Jesus' ministry was not so much in the sacred as out in the world where men bought and sold and dealt with the hard realities of life. George MacLeod has reminded us that Jesus Christ was not crucified in a cathedral between two candles, but on a cross between two thieves.

The language of Jesus was not that of the synagogue and temple. His language was drawn from the common life. It was secular language. Amos Wilder has reminded us that "the founder of Christianity used the language and idioms of the people, not sacred or holy language, nor a learned language, nor did they encourage an ecstatic language."[5]

Second, Biblical faith and secularity put great responsibility in man's hands for his world and history. Secularity calls man to be responsible, creative, courageous, and humanitarian. If he succeeds in his fulfillment, he is to be praised. If he fails, he alone is to be blamed. Secularity sees man's responsibility for his destiny in an absolute sense, while Biblical faith does not. Yet, Biblical faith and secularity have much in common here. God has entrusted much to

5. Op. cit., p. 26

man. Man is to be the master of his earth and responsible for his history. He has been given "dominion over the fish of the sea and over the birds of the air and over every living thing that moves upon the earth." (Gen. 1:28, RSV). Man has been created a little less than God and God has given him dominion over the works of his hands (Psa. 8). He must not ask God to do for him what he can do for himself. If, in his pride and selfishness, man creates war, allows poverty, pollutes his earth, sanctions racism and social injustice in its many forms, he must accept responsibility for these. He cannot blame God or fate. Man is responsible and is capable of accomplishing much that is good in his history.

Third, a close relationship between Biblical faith and secularity is seen in the fact that secularity with its science and technology arose from the culture that has been most influenced by the Biblical faith; namely, Western Europe and the United States. There is a reason for this and the reason seems to be that the nature of the world and man's place in it is most clearly seen through the eye of Biblical faith. The natural order is not sacral and unchanging, and it is not under the control of gods, demi-gods, and demons. Nature is a created order, being under the ultimate control of God but in a more immediate sense under the control of man. Therefore, nature is open to man's probing inquiry and mastery. Only in such a context could modern science and technology have risen. Secularity should not forget from whence it has come and why it comes from this particular source.

Fourth, that secularity is often a secularized version of Biblical faith is seen in the fact that secularity has followed in the wake of Christian missions. Christian missionaries have been, especially in Asia and Africa, the agents of secularity, although they did not intend it nor were aware of it. Lesslie Newbigin has made this observation: "The process of secularization in India is accomplishing the kind of changes in patterns of human living for which Christian missionaries fought with such stubborn perseverance a century and a half ago—the abolition of untouchability, the dowry system, of temple prostitution, the spread of education and medical service, and so on. . . . The ideas of human dignity, or social justice, of the significance of human history, which missionaries brought with them in their teaching of the Bible, have now become the property of those who claim no Christian allegiance, and the effect of these ideas is to discredit much that was formally protected by traditional religion."[6]

The modern preacher must not, therefore, see secularization as the sworn enemy of the Christian gospel. He has a point of contact with the secularists and often he finds friendship there, although it may be more in disguise than obvious. Jesus Christ must feel more at home with dedicated secularists doing a hard fight for human dignity and justice in the inner city than in a suburban church that is in bondage to its society, defending the status quo, and preaching the gospel of its culture more than the gospel of Jesus Christ.

Beyond Secularity

In preaching to secular man, we have to be open to him and accept him. We have to listen to him. And our listening must be more than a formality. We should listen to him in order to learn from him. He has much to teach us. The concern of the dedicated secularist for human dignity, human betterment and social justice must be ours. These are among the concerns of the gospel we preach. We cannot be dogmatic and judgmental. If we are, we miss our chance with him. Our authority cannot be in pounding the pulpit and a thunderous "thus saith the Lord." Our authority must be in the love of Christ that has become incarnate in us, issuing in service to men. Yet, we must point beyond secularity. Secularity is not enough. It cannot meet the deepest needs of man's life nor give adequate meaning to his existence. There is a reality that eludes it. The modern preacher, therefore, must point beyond secularity for at least four reasons.

First, there is a dimension beyond man. Man is born into an order which he did not create. He is not the source of his own life nor the sole master of his end and destiny.

William Hamilton tells about being on his back lawn one night with his young son. The sky was particularly brilliant that evening. He remembered how awe-struck he was by the heavens when he was a lad about his boy's age. He felt mystery and wonder in them. But his son, in a most matter-of-fact way, pointed to the heavens and said: "There is where we put our satellites." Wonder and mystery were missing from his life.

It is true that man does put his satellites into the heavens. But

---

6. Op. cit., pp. 17-18

the important thing is that he didn't put the heavens there. He did not create space with its planets, suns, and stars. Our universe has a Creator who was not man.

Secular man is lacking in mystery and wonder. Therefore, he is slow to worship. There are no vaulted archways over his life. His ceilings are often oppressively low.

Secular man has exchanged one myth for another. He has exchanged the myth of a three-story universe for the myth of a one-story universe. Everything moves on a horizontal plane. That is a myth, too. His life has height and depth of which he is not aware.

It is true that man has been made to fulfill his life in his brother. Real individuality and personal integrity are made possible only in social relations. They are not realized in isolation. They are not achieved by gazing at one's face in the mirror. Life is fulfilled in the brother. We are made for compassion, service, and justice. The secularist knows this. But what he fails to realize is that man also finds fulfillment in mystery, adoration, praise, and worship. There is a claim laid upon his life from beyond him. Man must also fulfill his life in God.

The Creator is more than a cosmic engineer. He is more like a father with love and compassion. He is concerned about us in our struggle for human betterment. The Creator has entered our arena of human struggle in somebody like ourselves. His entrance was not an invasion from outer space. It was qualitative rather than spacial. His love, which is healing and redemptive, found unique expression in Jesus Christ. A man's response to Jesus Christ is of first importance, although such a response and the response he makes to his brother are not mutually exclusive in any sense.

Second, the dignity of man must have a more adequate basis than secularity can give.

The question is: Is man a child of nature or a child of God? Has man been cast up by nature or created by God? Is he organized vitalities of nature or does he have something of the nature of God in him? Does he have only a biological and chemical imprint upon his life or does he have the image of God? Biblical faith affirms that, while man is grounded in nature, he gets his worth and dignity from God who has made him and loves him.

Historian Arnold J. Toynbee has reminded us that man keeps his humanity only as he believes in God. When he ceases to believe in God, he ceases to be human. He becomes something less than man.

Harvey Cox has written of the same thing: "One must be responsible for something before someone. Man, in order to be free and responsible, which means to be man, must answer to that which is not man."[7]

If man is rooted in nothing but nature and is responsible to no one but himself, how will he be saved from being used, manipulated and exploited? There is not sufficient dignity about him to be kept inviolate.

Third, secularity takes too lightly the problem of evil. It does not take evil with a seriousness commensurate with its reality. Evil is found within man's personal life as well as his corporate life. It is more real, more intransigent, and more tragic than secularity knows.

Langdon Gilkey, observing our inability to follow the ethical image of Jesus, has written. "Something in ourselves that we perhaps did not know was there, prevents our enactment of this image; we seem unable perhaps even strangely unwilling, to become what we thought we really wanted to be."[8] And we discover the same things in others. Gilkey continues: "Or, to be honest, it is our most common experience of others: It is perfectly evident to all of us that these others do not live up to their ideals. We see this in our roommate or a professional colleague telling us about cherished goals."[9]

But man in his corporate life does even worse. As has already been observed, as a member of the community, the corporation, or the army, he will do things that he would not think of doing in personal relationships.

Only the gospel can take evil seriously and not yield to despair. It can still hope because it knows of forgiveness, reconciliation, and renewal offered in Jesus Christ. Jesus Christ is more than one who presses ethical demands upon us. If this were what He did essentially, He would be the worst moral despot history has known. His ethical burden would be intolerable. Jesus Christ is Savior and Redeemer.

Fourth, secularity cannot give adequate renewal for moral fatigue. The secularist often experiences moral fatigue resulting

7. Harvey Cox, *The Secular City* (New York: The Macmillan Company, 1965), p. 259
8. Op. cit., p. 385
9. Ibid., p. 386

from frustration of effort, and his moral fatigue can easily pass into cynicism and despair.

Frequently the idealistic secularist is frustrated in his effort. He finds structures of power with injustice more unyielding than he knew, minds steeped more deeply in prejudice than he was aware, human inertia more massive than he realized, and people whose causes he had championed often unappreciative and unresponsive. He grows tired.

I remember the students at the college where my son was a freshman who were striking in protest when American troops invaded Cambodia. He called me that night to tell me about the idealism of the protest sweeping the campus and urged me to do all I could in my community for the cause of immediate peace. Students were allowed to leave school and engage in political, and other appropriate action, to change public opinion about the war. They could complete their work the following fall without penalty. One of the first things my son told me upon returning home for the summer was how the idealism and concern finally degenerated into long hours at the bridge table. He was discovering how hard it is to keep idealistic and vigorous action sustained. Weariness overtakes men.

Moral fatigue can end in cynicism and despair, as is well illustrated by H. G. Wells. He was a humanist who, during his early years and middle life, had great hopes for men. Through man's rationality with his science and technology, human progress seemed to come almost inevitably upon us. But as an old man he was exhausted and in utter despair. The universe was bankrupt, man was at the end of his tether, and the human story was washed up. There was no hope.

The Christian has a resource of renewal that the secularist knows nothing about. Through his faith, he sees man's inhumanity cutting across the grain of a moral universe. There is a moral order which opposes such action and upon which all forms of social injustice must at last destroy themselves. But beyond that, God is not morally neutral. He has set Himself against all forces that degrade and dehumanize persons, and He has promised to renew those who wait upon Him. The Christ of the Christian gospel has invited the weary to come to Him for rest. He has promised to give them strength and to be with them to the end of the age.

The modern preacher faces no greater challenge than that of ministering and preaching to secular man. But he need not despair. There is hope!

15 / PREACHING TO COSMIC MAN

A PREACHER MUST BE AWARE OF THE MOOD OF HIS TIME. HE DOES not preach the mood but he must preach to that mood. The gospel must be addressed to the living and vital concerns of his generation. Unless the preacher can do this, he and his generation will not make contact.

Moods of history do not validate or invalidate Christian truth. But moods of history throw certain Christian truths into focus and call forth their relevance.

One of the dominant moods of our time is what we can call the cosmic mood. This mood is certain to throw the church's doctrine of the cosmic Christ into a new focus and show its relevance in a way never before experienced in the history of modern preaching. We are called upon to preach the cosmic Christ to cosmic man.

The Cosmic Mood

Cosmic man has emerged in our time. Our astronauts' orbital flight of the moon during Christmas of 1968 marked a new era, a new beginning for man. Man did a thing he had never done before: He went beyond earth's atmosphere and beyond the gravitational field of earth. He reached that point for the first time in history where earth no longer pulled him back to herself. Earth seemed to release him to the larger universe. And man became a new kind of man. Until then he had always been earth-bound. But in that historic flight he became cosmic man.

The Russians call their space fliers cosmonauts while we call our space fliers astronauts. The term cosmonaut literally means "sailor of the cosmos." The meaning of astronaut is even more poetical and beautiful. It means "sailor of the stars." The man who can be spoken of as sailor of the cosmos or sailor of the stars is obviously cosmic man.

John F. Kennedy used the same metaphor when he was urging our nation to explore space. He exhorted us to "set sail on this new sea." The new sea is the sea of space, the cosmic sea.

With the emergence of cosmic man comes the cosmic mood. Modern man is cosmically oriented. He thinks cosmically, hopes cosmically, and plans cosmically. He is prepared to live cosmically. Man is no longer tethered to his earth. He is prepared to live beyond his earth. He has walked on the moon, and he dreams of even greater exploits. While there will likely never be a great exit from earth to planets of space, man will be very aware of the cosmic dimension of his living.

We have been very conscious of history as being the place of God's revelation. We have not found God so much in nature. Nor have we found Him mystically or rationally in any basic sense. We have looked to history for God's disclosure of Himself. We have seen God in His mighty acts among men. We have seen Him supremely in the historic person of Jesus Christ. Being so historically oriented, the doctrine of the cosmic Christ has often seemed to be an embarrassing intrusion into our theology and preaching. But the present cosmic mood opens a door for the preaching of the cosmic Christ in a way not experienced in our time.

The Cosmic Christ

The New Testament presents Jesus Christ as historic and earthbound, but it also presents Him as cosmic, free from earth's limitation of space and time. There are five great doctrines that represent Christ as being cosmic.

The cosmic Christ is reflected in the doctrine of creation. Christian faith does not believe that our universe is the result of blind chance and accident. Our universe was born of purpose because it had a Creator. The New Testament makes this staggering claim: The pre-existent Christ was the agent of creation. "All things were made by him, and without him was not anything made that was made" (John 1:3). "For in him all things were created, in heaven and on earth, visible and invisible, whether thrones or dominions or principalities or authorities—all things were created through him and for him" (Col. 1:16, RSV). "But in these last days he has spoken to us by a Son, whom he appointed the heir of all things, through whom also he created the world" (Heb. 1:2, RSV).

The Resurrection points in the direction of the cosmic Christ. Jesus Christ was set free from death, which is the greatest tragedy of historical existence. Christ is seen moving from earth-boundness to cosmic freedom. He appeared suddenly and disappeared with the same suddenness. He transcends the limitations of earth's time and space.

The Ascension further clarifies the cosmic Christ. Christ was lifted up out of the sight of men. His ascension is described like this: ". . . as they were looking on, he was lifted up, and a cloud took him out of their sight" (Acts 1:9, RSV).

The Ascension does not mean that Christ ascended to the third story of a three story universe. He freed himself from earth-boundness. Yet, the meaning of the Ascension is not to be understood in terms of space essentially. It is concerned with the power and sovereignty of Christ.

The doctrine of the exalted Christ obviously represents Him as the cosmic Christ. "Therefore God also hath highly exalted him" (Phil. 2:9) . . . "far above all rule and authority and power and dominion, and above every name that is named, not only in this age but also in that which is to come, and he has put all things under his feet and has made him the head over all things for the church" (Eph. 1:21-22, RSV). He is as cosmic as God since God has "made him sit at his right hand in the heavenly places" (Eph. 1:20, RSV). But to be seated at the right hand of God does not mean to be seated on a throne somewhere in space. It means to be sovereign and to have ultimate power at His disposal.

Finally, the doctrine of reconciliation points to a Christ whose work of redemption brought cosmic results. Not only have earthly and human powers been reconciled to God through Christ, but hostile powers beyond earth have been reconciled to their Creator. Reconciliation has a cosmic dimension. Paul speaks about God's plan for the fullness of time which was "to unite all things in him [Christ], things in heaven and things on earth" (Eph. 1:10). God has reconciled to himself through Christ ". . . all things, whether on earth or in heaven, making peace by the blood of his cross" (Col. 1:20).

Preaching the Cosmic Christ

In preaching the cosmic Christ to cosmic man, the preacher must be sensitive to certain things.

First, the cosmic Christ must be preached to a paradoxical man —one who is conscious of power and achievement, yet feels overwhelmed by problems beyond his control.

There are two Biblical images of man. When man is contrasted with the eternal God, he is like the grass that wilts and the flower that fades. He is dust. But when seen in the light of his full potential that God has given him, man is a little less than his Creator, crowned with glory and honor, having dominion over the works of God's hands. Cosmic man feels both images in his life. He feels like grass before the scorching winds from the desert. Yet, he sees himself rising up to the full stature of his potential.

Man today turns toward the conquest of space with a sense of confidence Western Europe didn't have when it turned toward the new world at the close of the fifteenth century. The men who sailed with Columbus in 1492 were much more fearful and uncertain than the crew on Apollo 8. Many of the sailors begged Columbus to turn back, while others turned to mutiny. Some of the sailors were tied to the deck of the ship to keep them from irrational and destructive behavior. No one on Apollo 8 had that kind of mentality. Yet, we feel less secure about our future than did Columbus' generation.

Isaac Watts in one of his hymns asks: "Would he devote that sacred head for such a worm as I?" While being chastened by his growing sense of helplessness, cosmic man is too conscious of his power and achievement to be addressed in such a lowly manner. The preacher must preach the gospel so as to lift cosmic man out of a kind of fated existence, yet address him as one come of age, who is aware of his great power and notable achievements.

Second, the cosmic Christ must be preached to a man whose life is set within an ethical dualism.

The achievements of cosmic man have not set him free from an ethical dualism which has threatened man through all his history. His phenomenal success in technology only makes this dualism more threatening than ever. Great creative forces and immense destructive powers are at odds within his life. Cosmic man can be more creative than any man before him or he can be more destructive than any man of history.

Man's history on earth has been a story of glory and tragedy. He has produced great music, great art, great literature, and great systems of thought. He has been humane and heroic. He has often achieved real community, great goodness, and commendable justice. He has often truly worshiped God and offered to God the best his hands and mind have created. This has been his glory.

But tragedy has dogged his footsteps and marred his history. Man has been afflicted with bias, anxiety, prejudice, and hatred. He has had overwhelming pride and lust for power. Drunk with power he has sometimes claimed to be a master race with the prerogative of making inferior men his slaves. He has claimed rights for himself that only God possesses. Often in fear and anger he has dashed to pieces the best his hands and mind have created. He has been destructive and he has killed. This has been his tragedy.

All of man's history until now has been earth-bound. For the first time he is now able to project his history beyond earth. Will he colonize some inhabitable planet? Yes, possibly. Will he take his earth-bound as well as his heightened cosmic glory there? Yes, likely. And will he carry his tragedy? Will he take his bias, prejudice, overwhelming pride, and his lust for power? Will he throw up barriers that separate him from his fellows? Will men under the delusion of being a master race seek to enslave other men on some far-off planet? Will man fight for land, power and prestige there? Will he kill and destroy? The possibility of this is one of the shadows that lies across his cosmic future.

The crucial question is: How will cosmic man use his immense power? Will he choose to live on earth yet think cosmically, or will he shuttle back and forth between earth and beyond earth, or will he live beyond his earth?

President Kennedy in his inaugural address said: "For man holds in his mortal hands the power to abolish all forms of human poverty and all forms of human life." This is still the truth, yet it is much more crucial today than it was when President Kennedy spoke it.

Cosmic man is in trouble. Whether he lives on earth with a cosmic orientation or inhabits planets in space, he is in great need. He needs moral power he does not possess to control his awesome technological power. He needs social dedication which he does not have to enable him to live for the common good and welfare of all men. Yes, and he needs forgiveness for sins. He needs salvation. He needs redemption more than any man before him. This is so, not necessarily because he is more sinful than other men have been, but because the destructive possibilities of his life are so much greater. The astronaut needs redemption as much, even more, than Palestinian shepherds about whom Jesus spoke. The cosmonaut needs redemption as much, even more, than the camel driver.

Third, an unlimited cosmic Christ is preached to limited cosmic man.

We must remember that while Christ is cosmic in some ultimate sense, man is cosmic in a limited sense. Christ is no more limited by space and time than God is. Christ is seated at the right hand of God, the place of illimitable and sovereign power. But man is not free of space and time. He is capable of freeing himself from earth's space and time, but he can never transcend space and time in any ultimate sense. Wherever he goes he is still in space, being subject to it, and he is never free from some time system.

Fourth, in our preaching the historic Jesus will be the clue to the cosmic Christ.

Just as earth will be cosmic man's point of reference since earth is his home, so the point of reference for the cosmic Christ is the Jesus Christ we have known in our history. The clue to the cosmic Christ is the historic Jesus who took children into His arms, healed blind eyes, unstopped deaf ears, was a friend of sinners, loved the unlovely, opposed bigotry and pretension in all forms, and laid down His life for the sins of the world. The cosmic Christ is not somebody we have not known. He is the historic Jesus we have known, set free from the limits of time and space, with sovereign power in His hands. The historic Jesus is the key that unlocks the vast mystery, goodness, love, mercy and power of the cosmic Christ.

We preach the cosmic Christ as the hope for cosmic man. It is He who can humble man's pride, purge his lust for power, and resolve his conflict in peace. It is this Christ who can give him moral strength adequate for control of his technological power and a social dedication which will enable him to live beyond his private ambition for the common good of men. And the cosmic Christ can forgive the sins of cosmic man and reconcile him to God.